WITH

*A Behavioural
Analysis of Sport*

A Behavioural Analysis of Sport

by

JOHN DICKINSON, *PhD*

Simon Fraser University
Burnaby, British Columbia, Canada

PRINCETON BOOK COMPANY, PUBLISHERS
Princeton, New Jersey 1977

ISBN 0 86019 014 5

Princeton Book Company Edition 1977
Printed in the United States of America by Haddon Craftsmen

The Author

John Dickinson is an Associate Professor in the Department of Kinesiology, Simon Fraser University, Burnaby, British Columbia, Canada. He moved to this position in 1976 having previously been Associate Professor in the Psychology Department of St. Francis Xavier University. He received his Ph.D. in Psychology from Nottingham University, England.

Contents

Preface

During the last ten years there has been a remarkable development of interest in the field of Sports Psychology. This is evidenced in the formation of both national and international societies and in the publication of journals and books dealing with the topic. Despite the mounting interest, this field of applied study is still very much in its infancy. One of the effects of this immaturity is a tendency to eclecticism. Most books concerning the psychology of sport attempt to provide explanations or descriptions of sports behaviours on the basis of whatever psychological approaches appear appropriate. Humanist, cognitive, experimental, behaviourist and psychoanalytic viewpoints may be invoked in the same text as explanations for different aspects of sports activity. Eclecticism has much to recommend it in a new field of applied study. Alternative theoretical frameworks can be applied to a specific aspect of behaviour and their relative merits may be assessed. The disadvantages of this approach lie in the absence of any unifying conception of the field in its totality and in a tendency towards superficiality. This book represents an attempt at reversing this trend. The phenomenon of sport in society is described in terms of a single psychological approach. Sport is examined using the conceptualisation of behaviour as propounded by B.F. Skinner.

Skinner's work on operant conditioning in infrahuman organisms was concerned initially with the formulation and testing of principles governing the acquisition and maintenance of relatively simple responses in simplified environmental contexts. It soon became apparent to Skinner and his co-workers that the principles they discovered were relevant to the behaviour of man in all the complexity of his interaction with his environment. Over the last thirty years Skinner's laboratory research has continued, but his preoccupation has been with the application of his behavioural principles to education specifically and to societal change in general. His early views were summarized in *Science and Human Behaviour* (1953) whose impact was mainly on the community of academic psychologists. The publication of Skinner's novel *Walden Two* (1948) and his recent work *Beyond Freedom and Dignity* (1971) brought his views before the general public. The latter work described current world problems in terms of Skinner's principles of behaviour and suggested that the solution to the problems lay in the development of an adequate behavioural technology.

This book takes the same approach to one small aspect of behaviour in our society and describes it in Skinnerian terms. It attempts the identification of the environmental contingencies of reinforcement and punishment which lead to participation in sports, the effect of these contingencies on the acquisition of skills and the social behaviours with which sports are associated. The book should be regarded as a controversial starting point in the attempt to form a unifying framework in which the psychology of sport may develop. It is hoped that those concerned with sport will find this treatment stimulating and I should welcome comments and criticisms of the book.

I am indebted to Dr. B.F. Skinner for the inspiration for this book. My colleagues in the Psychology Department have supported this work with their interest and encouragement and I am grateful to St. Francis Xavier University's Council of Research for financial assistance in its completion.

John Dickinson
St. Francis Xavier University
Antigonish, Nova Scotia
Canada
1975

Section One   *Skinnerian Behaviourism*

Introduction

The stimulation for this book came from B.F. Skinner's work, *Beyond Freedom and Dignity*. In this manifesto, Skinner applied the principles of behaviour, derived from many years of experimental research, to the current state of social man and his struggle for survival in the face of threats from nuclear warfare, overpopulation and the depletion of his environment. His book examined the current state of the world and described it in behavioural terms. The description was followed by a prescription for a new society in which a behavioural technology would be developed, capable of resolving those problems which threaten man's existence. He suggested that the goal of survival may be achieved by application of the principles of behaviour discovered in laboratory work with animals and men and already applied in miniature in real-life situations.

Although many principles are already understood and could be applied. in rather straightforward fashion, his book also constituted a plea for further research in order for a behavioural technology to be developed adequate to the needs of a highly complex society.

Of necessity, Skinner's analysis and prescriptions were generalizations since he attempted the examination of the whole of society. No doubt it is his intention that others should investigate specific aspects of our culture in the light of the principals he expounds. In this book, I have taken one aspect of behaviour in our culture and attempted to describe the phenomenon in Skinnerian terms. The products of the analysis lead to some prescriptions for change and these are offered tentatively as a basis for discussion.

Beyond Freedom and Dignity aroused a great deal of controversy. The idea of behavioural technology and control of human behaviour, even when the objectives are universally acceptable, proved anathema to many and his critics have been vociferous in their condemnation of both his world-view and his prescriptions for a new society. One author (Platt, 1973) has likened Skinner to Darwin:

> The comparison with Darwin is not inappropriate. Both men started from a small set of problems and forced a radical rethinking of everything else in the field. Both men displaced the old verbal explanations with an almost mechanical description of basic processes of life and man . . . And in both cases, in spite of the scientific clarification and the technical successes, there were loud protests from the defenders of humanism and morality.

1

Skinner's basic view of behaviour is very simply described, but its implications for our conception of man are so far-reaching that the polemics are not surprising. According to Skinner, the behaviour of organisms is a function of three factors; their history of reinforcement and punishment, the stimuli which impinge upon them at any one moment and their state of deprivation. It is this fundamental concept of the nature of behaviour which we shall use in our discussion of sport. Later sections of this work consider the details of behavioural analysis, but some of the implications of this view can be discussed here.

If we accept that all behaviours can be explained on the basis of these three factors, we are, thereby, accepting that human behaviour is lawful and predictable. It is also implicit that behaviour can be manipulated. These corollaries to the Skinnerian view have led many to believe that Skinner is making a denial of 'free-will'. Rozynko et al (1973) have called this central controversy a pseudo-problem:

> If freedom and free will are synonymous with whimsy or are independent from any parameters in the environment — past or present, internal or external — then Skinner's system negates freedom. On the other hand, if freedom means the existence of a multitude of alternatives for behaviour, which at any instant may occur lawfully to result in a specific response, then there is no conflict.

It is only our ignorance concerning the history of an individual and his current state of deprivation which may lead us to assume that his behaviour is capricious or unpredictable. Once we accept that it is what an organism's environment has done to him in the past and what it is currently doing to him, which results in his producing particular behaviours, we can then direct our research towards discovering the relationship between a bit of behaviour and its history of reinforcement and subsequently change that behaviour by changing its consequences.

In a Skinnerian analysis of behaviour, the internal and unobservable causes of behaviour are dismissed as being prescientific. Their continued use is also positively harmful, since the 'explanations' of behaviour which they provide retard the search for the relationship between the environment and behaviour and consequently prevent the appropriate manipulation of that behaviour. When man abrogates to himself intentions, freedom, dignity, responsibility and will, he neglects to examine the environment which supplied the contingencies of reinforcement which produced the behaviour. For example, we give people credit for being honest and condemn those who are dishonest as though these traits were innate or the product of some internal process. We imply that people are free to choose to be one or the other. It is both more productive and valuable to ask what history of reinforcement contingencies produced honest *behaviour* in one individual and dishonest *behaviour* in another. If this question is answered, it provides both a description of the behaviour and the means by

2

which the behaviour may be changed. By altering the reinforcement contingencies of the individual it is possible that we shall change his behaviour or, more convincingly, so arrange the contingencies that another child will produce honest rather than dishonest behaviour.

It is this determinism which, as part of Skinner's description of the world, has brought him much opprobrium from the critics. By explaining human behaviour in terms of the impact of a changeable environment, Skinner develops the theme that our behaviour is the product of our experience at the hands of the environment and the most salient aspect of this environment, its reinforcing potential.

Since we have developed the tendency of attributing much of our behaviour to internal sources, society has been very negligent in planning the contingencies of reinforcement for behaviour. It would be far better, Skinner argues, to accept the fact of determinism, to plan the kinds of behaviours we wish to see in society, and then develop the reinforcement contingencies or environmental consequences which produce those behaviours. Once we have eradicated the explanations of behaviour based on causes internal to the individual, we can make progress in the development of a behavioural technology.

Skinner calls the 'person inside the person' the autonomous man. He is regarded as autonomous in the sense that his behaviour is believed to be uncaused. This concept of man is slowly being eroded and we no longer hold people 'responsible' for their actions in many situations. We accept that the environment of the ghetto child must, at least partly, bear the responsibility for the fact that he turns to crime. Nevertheless, in a large proportion of cases we still acknowledge autonomous man and, holding him responsible for his actions, we justifiably punish him for his unacceptable behaviours. In the analysis of sport it is perhaps more relevant to emphasize the fact that, just as the abolition of autonomous man places responsibility for inappropriate actions on the environment so does his abolition shift the credit for his successes to the environment. Superior performance in sport is often reinforced by praise and esteem. As soon as we recognize that the performance is a result of environmental factors over which the subject has no control, we detract from this esteem. In Skinner's words, 'To give a person credit for winning a game is to emphasize the fact that the victory was contingent on something he did, and the victory may then become more reinforcing to him.' (Skinner, 1971, p. 42). The reduction in credit for performance is one aspect of Skinner's work which has created a good deal of controversy. He points out that much of the ' . . . literature of dignity is concerned with preserving due credit,' and that the scientific analysis of behaviour is bound to meet with opposition since, 'A scientific conception seems demeaning because nothing is eventually left for which autonomous man can take credit.'

The literature of sport is replete with explanations involving autonomous man. If we are to analyze the phenomenon of sport in Skinnerian terms, we must translate these explanations into acceptable scientific accounts of behaviour based on the conditions which have influenced an individual during

3

his lifetime or based on the genetic endowment which, as a member of the species, is a result of the evolutionary process and hence, a product of the conditions under which the species has developed.

At this point we may give just a few examples of the translations which are necessary. Frequently we hear that a performer's success in sport is due to his determination, his grit, his gifts or his competitiveness. These explanations are meaningless. If we observe a set of behaviours in an individual which appear in his repertoire of response with some frequency, we may use a short-hand description of those behaviours by subsuming them under a single label. If an individual trains hard for a long period of time without receiving much reward, gives up other activities in order to do this, verbally proclaims he will some day succeed, we are likely to give these behaviours, in total, the label 'determination'. If the individual does eventually succeed, it is tempting to say it is *because* of his determination. But the explanation explains nothing about the behaviours and refers us only to a hypothetical internal characteristic. We have described his behaviour in short-hand form and now use the short-hand to explain his behaviour. We attribute his success to autonomous man. What we need to know are the antecedent conditions which produce those specific behaviours in that individual. When we have this information our explanation becomes fruitful, because we can so arrange conditions that these behaviours are produced by others, if they are desirable. Reification, the process of explaining by giving a label, has been common in psychology and is also found in sport. Nowhere is this process more obvious than in the use of the label 'natural athlete'. An individual learns many skills quickly and our short-hand description for this behaviour is that he is a natural athlete. When he begins another new skill and learns that quickly too, we hear it said that he has done so *because* he is a natural athlete. All this is tantamount to saying is that he learns skills quickly *because* he learns quickly. Obviously the explanation is totally pointless.

The insidious aspect of the pseudoexplanation is that it terminates curiosity. He is successful in sport because of a 'will to achieve' is an apparent explanation for a bit of behaviour. In fact it has no basis whatsoever, merely referring us to a supposed internal cause, but the apparent explanatory function of the statement is superficially satisfying. Instead we should be asking, what are the behaviours which led to success and what are the environmental determinants of those behaviours.

Repeatedly in the literature of sport, performances are credited to some aspect of autonomous man. Only by seeking the environmental determinants of behaviour can we begin to predict behaviour accurately and manipulate the environment so that the desirable behaviours are produced.

Many of the explanations of sports behaviour consist of references to motivation. Coaching manuals often devote chapters to the 'raising of motivation' or the maintenance of 'high motivation' during a season of play. In our threefold analysis of behaviour the question of motivation is summarized in the final part: the organism's state of deprivation. In large measure, in both experimental studies where a controlled state of deprivation is produced in the

4

animals and in many human situations, the level of deprivation of an organism is relatively unimportant. Furthermore, it may be misleading to consider motivation as a causal factor. In an excellent brief treatment of motivation, Reynolds (1968) makes the following point:

> . . . the problem of inaction in a particular situation is commonly explained as a lack of motivation. If the organism were motivated, it would behave, and, moreover, would behave correctly (if, of course, the motivation were not too great). This sort of explanation does no more than give a commonsense reason for the occurrence or nonoccurrence of behaviour. It gives no indication of the controlling variables. It is thus inherently useless. Moreover, it may be in error. If the inaction is occasioned by the early part of a fixed-interval schedule of reinforcement, it is incorrect to attribute it to a lack of motivation.

The error, Reynolds contends, can lead to misdirected attempts to modify the behaviour. If the situation described above is brought about by a fixed-interval schedule of reinforcement, it is a change in the schedule which is required. Motivational variables, such as states of deprivation, are not relevant. Attempts to manipulate these variables are, therefore, doomed to failure.

We can apply this example very easily to sport. Many aspects of sports behaviour receive some of their reinforcement on a fixed-interval basis. Regular competition and its associated rewards, are equivalent to fixed-interval schedules. We should not be surprised to find that following a competition, there is a period of time in which no responding occurs. Reference to a drop in motivation is misleading, since it would lead us to attempt to manipulate the motivation of the competitors when all that is required is an alteration in the schedule of reinforcements. Obviously, this is a simplified version of the real-life situation. As we shall see, the reinforcements available for sports behaviour form a complex structure, many segments of which may reinforce on different schedules. However, the example illustrates the point that reference to motivational concepts can be entirely misleading. Only where states of deprivation are different can we use these concepts in an explanatory way concerning differences in behaviour.

A frequent distinction is made between drive motivation and incentive motivation. Logan (1969) distinguished between these two forms in the following way:

> Drive motivation refers to the internal source of energy driving the organism to do something. . . . Many of these are based upon biological needs; organisms are impelled to reduce drives. Incentive motivation refers to the organism's expectation of reward for making a particular response.

In terms of sport this point of view might lead us to conclude that an

5

individual deprived of exercise may be more likely to undertake a sports activity and his expectation of success would act as an incentive. It is more parsimonious, however, to relate the individual's behaviour to his history of reinforcement for participation rather than any future expectation. Similarly, the drive motivation explanation does not appear valuable, since the ones who participate most frequently do not seem to be those who are most deprived of exercise. At a superficial level this motivational analysis does not appear to be particularly applicable. The argument might be made that the drives described are not appropriate and alternative possibilities will be discussed in later sections.

If one examines the chapters in those manuals which claim to provide ways to manipulate the motivation of individuals very little concrete advice is presented. In large measure the advice is concerned simply with the manipulation of consequences of the behaviour of the performer. Give praise, provide competition, diversify the training program, appear as common alternatives. What is suggested is the manipulation of the environment and not some internal characteristic. These independent variables may result in changes of behaviour and our explanation of those changes can be made in a very straightforward fashion with reference to the independent variables; the environment. The conception of a change in internal state is redundant, an explanatory fiction which detracts from our research into the determining variables.

The intention in this book is to explore some of the basic principles of behaviour which have been derived from the study of operant conditioning and to consider the phenomenon of sport in society in the light of these principles. It is hoped that this discussion provides some answers to the following questions. Why do people participate in sports? Why do some fail to participate in sports? How are the skills necessary for sports acquired?

One of the major difficulties in writing a book of this kind is the choice of language. In the last paragraph I used terminology which indicates a conception of man which is antithetical to a behavioural viewpoint. The phrase 'the intention in this book. . .' is exactly the kind of statement which Skinnerians regard as obsolete and meaningless. If behaviour is environmentally determined the term 'intention' has no value. Skinner faced a similar problem in writing *Beyond Freedom and Dignity* and made the following apology which also applies here:

> The text will often seem inconsistent. English like all languages, is full of prescientific terms which usually suffice for purposes of casual discourse. No one looks askance at the astronomer when he says that the sun rises or that stars come out at night, for it would be ridiculous to insist that he should always say that the sun appears over the horizon as the earth turns or that the stars become visible as the atmosphere ceases to refract sunlight. All we ask is that he can give a more precise translation if one is needed. . . . No doubt many of the mentalistic expressions embedded in the English language cannot be as rigorously translated as 'sunrise,' but acceptable translations are not out of reach.

Before beginning the discussion of sport, it is necessary that some of the terms used in a behavioural analysis are defined and explained. Many of the terms are common to everyday language, but are used in far more rigorous fashion by the psychologist. Although the terms themselves are of value, we must also examine some of the major experimental findings from research in operant conditioning.

A Definition of Terms
Operant Conditioning

In its narrowest sense operant conditioning refers to a process in which the frequency with which some aspect of behaviour occurs is changed by what happens after the behaviour is produced. In non-technical terms, operant conditioning usually refers to the modification of behaviour through the application of rewards and punishments. In a broader sense, operant conditioning has come to refer to an entire approach to psychology. The important relationship in operant conditioning is that between behaviour and the environment. In this context, the term environment is used with wider application than lay-usage. Environment, in operant conditioning terminology, includes not only the physical situation in which an organism is located, but the whole of the stimuli which may impinge upon an organism within that situation. Thus, other people with whom we are in contact are part of our environment and what they say and what they do to us or give us, are all part of the environment.

The other side of the relationship also needs some clarification. What is meant by behaviour? In discussions of operant conditioning we are most frequently concerned with what could be called voluntary behaviour. In other words, whether the behaviour occurs is not due to some specific eliciting stimulus, as is the case with a reflex. The behaviour is emitted rather than elicited. If one accepts the operant conditioning paradigm therefore, behaviour, in this context, refers to those aspects of what an organism does which are under the control of their consequences, rather than being produced automatically by the presentation of a particular stimulus. This brief description suggests that many of our autonomic functions are not behaviour in Skinnerian terms. Increasingly it has been found that functions such as vasodilation, heart rate and blood pressure are amenable to modification through operant conditioning techniques. It may be the case that many bodily functions, over which we had considered voluntary control was impossible, may succumb to operant conditioning techniques. These research endeavours are of only passing interest in the light of the nature of this book. The majority of the behaviours to be discussed come within the scope of what are colloquially called voluntary.

Although there is a general distinction between voluntary and involuntary behaviour it is not a distinction based upon control or the absence of control:

The distinction between voluntary and involuntary behaviour is a matter of the *kind* of control. It corresponds to the distinction between eliciting and discriminative stimuli. The eliciting stimulus appears to be more

7

coercive. Its causal connection with behaviour is relatively simple and easily observed. This may explain why it was discovered first. The discriminative stimulus, on the other hand, shares its control with other variables so that the inevitability of its effect cannot be easily demonstrated. But when all relevant variables have been taken into account, it is not difficult to guarantee the result — to force the discriminative operant as inexorably as the eliciting stimulus forces its response (Skinner, 1953).

The Skinnerian view may be summarized by saying that a distinction between voluntary and involuntary behaviour is dependent upon the subtlety of environmental control rather than that one category of behaviour is caused and the other uncaused.

This point of view carries over in the discussion of differences between operant and respondent conditioning. In respondent conditioning, reflex activity or involuntary behaviour is brought under the control of some novel and hitherto neutral eliciting stimulus. The procedure varies in a number of ways from the operant methods and some distinction should be made. In respondent or classical conditioning two stimuli are presented in close temporal proximity. One of these elicits a response 'involuntarily' from the organism. The other stimulus is neutral with respect to that response. Repeated pairings of these stimuli cause the neutral stimulus to elicit either some fraction or the complete response produced to the other.

There are several points of distinction between this kind of conditioning and operant conditioning. The two stimuli are presented to the organism by the experimenter and are not in any way contingent upon what the animal does. In operant conditioning the second stimulus is contingent upon the production of the response. The probability of a conditioned response being produced initially in respondent conditioning must be zero (the first stimulus is defined as being neutral), whereas the probability of the intended conditioned response cannot be zero in instrumental conditioning since the second stimulus is contingent upon its production.

Although there have been numerous attempts to equate these two types of conditioning and no real concensus has been reached regarding their relationship, it is simplest to keep the concepts distinct. Although a distinction is appropriate, it is often the case that both types of conditioning may occur within a single situation. For example, we have referred to an individual achieving reward in the form of success for his participation in a sport. The success is contingent upon his behaviour. Within the same situation, there may be noxious stimuli which automatically elicit a fear response. Other and initially neutral stimuli in the context may come to elicit this response. In this case performance of the sport skill may be accompanied by an emotional response which has been produced through respondent conditioning.

Reinforcement
Perhaps no single term in the recent history of psychology has been quite so

difficult to define precisely as reinforcement. (Instinct is an exception.) The term refers to an operation or a process in which a particular kind of stimulation is presented to an organism. The stimulation itself is usually known as the reinforcer. A stimulus is only labelled as a reinforcer when the effect of its presentation is to make a preceding response more likely to occur. Therefore, it is usual to talk of the reinforcement of responses rather than the reinforcement of organisms. One distinction that has been made is that a response is reinforced whereas an organism may be said to be rewarded. There is some apparent circularity in the definition of reinforcement and it is this which has caused difficulty with the definition. A reinforcer is any subsequent stimulus which, when applied, is followed by an increase in the probability of the behaviour being emitted. If a stimulus increases the probability of a behaviour it is a reinforcer: that is, a reinforcer is a reinforcer. In an earlier work Skinner (1953) dealt with this problem in the following way:

> The only way to tell whether or not a given event is reinforcing to a given organism under given conditions is to make a direct test. We observe the frequency of a selected response, then make an event contingent upon it and observe any change in frequency. If there is a change, we classify the event as reinforcing to the organism under the existing conditions. There is nothing circular about classifying events in terms of their effects; the criterion is both empirical and objective. It would be circular, however, if we then went on to assert that a given event strengthens an operant *because* it is reinforcing. We achieve a certain success in guessing at reinforcing powers only because we have in a sense made a crude survey; we have gauged the reinforcing effect of a stimulus upon ourselves and assume the same effect upon others. We are successful only when we resemble the organism under study and when we have correctly surveyed our own behaviour. (Skinner, 1953).

Perhaps, rather than become involved in this problem, it is simplest to accept the definition in its operational form. Most often the terms reinforcement and reward may be regarded as synonymous.

The kind of reinforcement we have been describing is generally designated as positive reinforcement. It is the application of a particular stimulus that increases the probability of preceding behaviour. It is also possible to increase the likelihood of responses by terminating some noxious stimulus. In other words, an organism may be rewarded or reinforced by having some unpleasant aspect of the environment removed. This kind of reward is called negative reinforcement and is only slightly less common in everyday life than positive reinforcement.

Negative reinforcement should not be confused (though it frequently is) with punishment. Punishment refers to the presentation of an unpleasant stimulus after a response has occurred. A punished response may become less probable in the future, whereas a negatively reinforced response becomes more probable. In

9

essence, the distinction between the two concepts depends upon the temporal locus of the noxious stimulus. In negative reinforcement this stimulus precedes the response and is terminated after the response is made. In punishment, the stimulus is presented after the response. The stimulus may be identical in the two situations, but the influence upon the response is opposite. Punishment, in the context of operant conditioning, has an identical meaning to its lay-usage. It is an unpleasant or aversive aspect of the environment applied to an organism after it has produced a response.

We could illustrate these points very simply in the case of sports activity. There are frequently tangible rewards provided for excellence in sport; the individual receives a cup or money or status which reinforces those responses. On the other hand, if one's doctor repeatedly nags and threatens that if some exercise is not taken, dire results will occur, we may terminate this noxious state of affairs by indulging in some sports activity; our participation is negatively reinforced. If, having begun to participate we break a leg, the same response has received punishment.

Any reinforcer which is used to modify behaviour may depend for its effectiveness on the state or the organism at the time when it is applied. For example, the majority of work with positive reinforcement for animal behaviour has revolved around the use of food or water. If an animal is deprived of these commodities for a period of time they gain in their effectiveness as reinforcers. In the laboratory, animals may be deprived of food for twenty-four hours before the experimental sessions or, alternatively, be maintained at some percentage of their body-weight which is less than that under free-feeding conditions. The point is that for a satiated animal a particular stimulus may lose its reinforcing properties. Notwithstanding the variable effectiveness of these reinforcers, they share one common property. Their effectiveness as reinforcers does not depend upon the experience of the animal. For all hungry rats, food is reinforcing. For all thirsty rats, water is reinforcing. The same is true for sexual behaviour. The opportunity to copulate is reinforcing for a sex-deprived rat and, similarly, the opportunity to sleep is reinforcing for a sleep-deprived rat. The benefits of these aspects of the environment to the animal and their consequent reinforcing value do not have to be learned. However, when we look at reward systems used for man in society, we find a different system in operation altogether. The majority of at least western men are reinforced by stimuli whose value has been learned. Money is the obvious example. Money acquires reinforcing properties as we increase in our experience of the world. We speak, in lay terms, of teaching children the value of money. Similarly, human behaviour is frequently reinforced by praise or social approval. The value of praise is learned. We are neither born with this capacity to value praise nor does it simply mature in us with age, it is a product of our experience. Badges, diplomas, certificates, grades, examination results, gold stars, smiles, attention from others, prestige and status may all serve as reinforcers. These learned reinforcers are usually termed either conditioned or secondary reinforcers, whereas the unlearned variety are known as primary reinforcers.

10

Although the reinforcing properties of secondary reinforcers are acquired, their effectiveness in that role may be variable depending on the state of the organism. Analogous with the primary reinforcers, a few pennies may be an effective reinforcer with the ghetto child, whereas they might have little reinforcing value for the rich child. Our description of the situation might be that one of the organisms is in a deprived state and the other is not. A child may be deprived of attention and hence find any attention devoted to him by adults to be reinforcing. The antecendent behaviour is therefore likely to increase in its probability of occurrence in the future. Conversely, the child who receives attention constantly may not find this aspect of the environment particularly reinforcing.

Secondary reinforcers may also be found in animal behaviour and the development of secondary reinforcing power by an initially neutral stimulus may be studied within the laboratory. The procedure by which this is achieved is very straightforward. The presence of a neutral stimulus, in close temporal proximity with a primary reinforcer, is sufficient for that stimulus to acquire reinforcing characteristics. A light flashed concurrently with the presentation of food over a large number of trials will cause the light to act as a reinforcer on its own. New behaviours may then be reinforced on the basis of the light alone. It is also possible for any well-established secondary reinforcer to serve in the production of reinforcing capacities in another neutral stimulus. For example, a buzzer may be added to the environment in which the flashing light is acting as a reinforcer and eventually come to act as a reinforcer in its own right. The association between the two stimuli produces this reinforcing capacity in an automatic fashion.

In man, verbal mediators are probably important in the development of the reinforcing properties of a neutral stimulus. However, in many cases it is also possible to identify the relationship between an acquired secondary reinforcer and the primary reinforcer with which it was associated. For the sake of argument we could assume that a need for maternal affection is unlearned. Maternal affection may therefore act as a reinforcer. Associated with maternal affection are facial expressions, such as smiles or softly spoken words. These in turn may acquire their own reinforcing characteristics.

If a secondary reinforcer has been associated with many different forms of primary reinforcer, it is usually referred to as a generalized reinforcer. A learned reinforcer which has become generalized does not depend for its reinforcing property on the state of deprivation of the organism. Although we used the example of money and deprivation in rich and ghetto children, the relationship is not always so straightforward as these extreme cases. Money may be an effective reinforcer even to the wealthy. It is the most common of the generalized reinforcers.

It is important to emphasize at this point that behavioural analysis eschews the concept of intent and for sound reasons. The claim is made that an organism behaves in the way it does because that behaviour has been reinforced in the past. In lay language we are usually tempted to say that an organism behaves in

11

a particular way *in order* to achieve reinforcement. Thus the organism is described as bringing an intention to his behaviour. The fallacy in this lay explanation can be pointed out by a simple example. Rats may be trained to run mazes on the basis of positive primary reinforcement. When observing a well trained rat running a maze it is tempting to say that the animal is running *in order* to reach the food, but suppose that we substitute a cat for the food at the end of the maze. The rat would still set off and run to the goal box. If the end result were to be that the cat ate the rat, our explanation would sound rather foolish. The rat ran the maze *in order* to be eaten! A plausible explanation would be that the rat ran the maze because *in the past* it had been reinforced for so doing. The history of reinforcement contingencies is important and we do not need to refer to unmeasurable internal concepts such as intention in order to explain the behaviour.

The point may be well taken in terms of sport. If we are reinforced for our participation in sport by social approval and on one occasion this is not forthcoming, (perhaps we behave in an unsporting fashion and are condemned for that performance) our 'intention' serves no explanatory function for our behaviour. We produced the behaviour because, in the past, it had been reinforced with approval. We can make the same point with respect to negative reinforcement. If the sun is shining in our eyes at one end of the tennis court, we put on dark glasses, because, in the past, the noxious state has thereby been terminated. If the sun is really hot we may put on a hat for the same reason. It is the consequences of previous actions which are important.

In order for a stimulus to be regarded as a reinforcer it must also possess an additional quality. Reinforcers are said to be trans-situational. This means that in order to be classified as a reinforcer the stimulus must be capable of strengthening a wide variety, if not all of the operant responses of which the animal is capable. Therein lies an additional distinction between respondent and operant conditioning. The conditioned responses elicited in respondent conditioning are highly specific to the nature of the second stimulus. Pavlov's dogs were conditioned to salivate to the initially neutral stimulus of a bell. The second stimulus in this case was the meat powder provided. Salivation would not have been conditioned had the second stimulus been electric shock.

In considering reinforcements for sport, the magnitude of the reinforcement is often contingent upon some quantitative or qualitative dimension of the response. In the laboratory the amount of reinforcement is usually standardized and provided on the production of the appropriate response. It is possible, however, to manipulate reinforcement in the more lifelike fashion. That is, we can provide so-called correlated reinforcement. For example, if an animal is reinforced for running to a goal box we may provide greater amounts of reinforcement the slower the rate of running. In this way we can produce slow-running behaviour rather than fast running behaviour. The topography of a response is as much under the controlling effects of reinforcement as its occurrence or non-occurrence.

12

Schedules of reinforcement

We have talked so far as though each time a behaviour is produced it is reinforced. This is by no means the case and is not necessarily optimal either, as we shall see later. It is perfectly possible to reinforce a response only intermittently. Partial reinforcement of responses is an area to which considerable experimental effort has been devoted. A behaviour may both increase in frequency and be maintained on the basis of partial reinforcement. The schedules upon which this partial reinforcement is given may be very simple or extremely complex. At the simplest end of the scale, one may reinforce an organism on some fixed interval basis for example, every thirty seconds provided at least one response is made. Alternatively, a fixed ratio schedule can be used in which the organism receives reinforcement after a predetermined number of responses have been made. These schedules may be complicated by adding some variability. An organism may be reinforced *on average* every thirty seconds, but the range of interval may be from one to sixty seconds, for example. Or an animal may receive reinforcement on average after every ten responses, but the range may be very wide indeed. Recently, highly complex schedules of reinforcement have been investigated. Multiple schedules of reinforcement have been used which involve the successive presentations of variable and fixed schedules. Some compound schedules have been developed in which a single reponse is reinforced according to the requirements of two or more schedules at the same time, either when the demands of all schedules have been satisfied, or when any one of the demands has been met.

The schedules of reinforcement have been developed in order to examine the characteristics of responding they generate. In real life we are seldom rewarded for every response we make and the schedules of partial reinforcement may be very influential upon our behaviour. In sport, nobody wins all the time and the mixture of reinforcement and punishment will have a bearing upon tendency to perform. Similarly our behaviour is likely to be manipulated on the basis of more than one schedule of reinforcement operating concurrently. The boxer may receive some variable ratio of reinforcement in terms of winning but may acquire continuous reinforcement from a coach or colleagues and at the same time encounter inherent punishment in the sport. The complex schedules studied within the laboratory are an attempt to replicate these highly intricate reinforcement contingencies which exist in real life.

Shaping

In its narrowest application operant conditioning requires that the response is first emitted by the organism. Appropriate reinforcement may then be provided to increase the frequency of that desired behaviour. Two problems emerge from this application. Firstly, the desired behaviour may have a relatively low probability in the organism's repertoire. For the experimenter in the laboratory or the human adult faced with teaching a skill to children, it might be extremely time-consuming to wait for the desired response before the modification of behaviour can begin. Secondly, the desired response may not form part of the

13

organism's existing repertoire at all. Thus, it may have a probability of zero of occurrence and the experimenter or teacher remain with nothing to reinforce. In order to circumvent these problems, techniques of shaping have been developed in the laboratory. Shaping refers to the gradual change of behaviour through reinforcement until the desired response is finally achieved. In practice, this means that during the acquisition of a response a subject may be initially provided with reinforcement for any behaviour that resembles the desired response. Having established this behaviour, reinforcement may then be witheld until a closer approximation to the correct response is made. The trainer or experimenter, therefore, produces a series of successive approximations to the desired response, finally no more reinforcement is provided until the desired response is achieved.

The description of the shaping procedure appears superficially to be contradictory to our earlier contention that in operant conditioning, the probability of the desired response is never zero. The explanation is simply that in the procedure of shaping we progressively change the nature of the desired conditioned response so that our reinforcement is contingent upon a new variation of the present response which is one step closer to the ultimate behavioural goal. The probability of this next stage is never zero, or we would not have any response to reinforce.

Shaping is fundamental to the acquisition of all skills. No one begins in a sport with a perfect set of responses. The topography of responses is progressively modified until it approaches the sport skill. The rate at which the shaping occurs is highly dependent on the skill and a perfect response may never be achieved. Finer and finer adjustments to the response may be made throughout the life of the participant.

Extinction

Once the subject is behaving in the way in which the experimenter or trainer demands, that behaviour may then be maintained. If, however, the trainer terminates the reinforcement, the organism will carry on responding, often for very considerable periods of time. Eventually, in the absence of reinforcement, the behaviour will extinguish. If an organism no longer receives reinforcement for his behaviour that behaviour will eventually cease. It is tempting to draw a parallel with memory and say that the subject has forgotten the response. One aspect of the extinction process precludes this analogy. This is the phenomenon of spontaneous recovery. If the animal is removed from the experimental environment and allowed to rest for a period of time and subsequently returned to the experimental environment, the operant behaviour will begin again, even though no reinforcement is presented. The behaviour will eventually extinguish again, or if reinforcement is reintroduced, quickly return to its previous level of occurrence. An extinguished response is not necessarily lost forever therefore, but may reappear either spontaneously or as a function of the reintroduction of reinforcement. If the response occurs spontaneously after extinction, it never appears with the same strength as at the high point of the conditioning process, but is always rather weak and easily extinguished again.

Counter-conditioning and omission training

So far we have mentioned two distinctive methods of eradicating responses. A response may be punished and thus result in a lower probability of future occurrence or it may be extinguished by withholding reinforcement. There are alternatives to these methods which are known as counter-conditioning and omission training. In counter-conditioning the current response is eradicated by reinforcing some alternative incompatible response. It is a mixture of the reinforcement and extinction principles. The response to be eradicated is no longer reinforced and in its place an alternative is reinforced. Omission training is somewhat similar. We simply give positive reinforcement when the organism does nothing in a situation where previously an unwanted response occurred. Suppose that, in a skill situation, unnecessary movement is made by a performer. That unnecessary movement may eventually extinguish because, when it is included, performance is poor and the total response is not reinforced. However, it may be more convenient and efficient to eliminate the movement by reinforcing its omission.

Stimulus control

For the vast majority of behaviours the probability with which a given response occurs may be manipulated by reinforcement contingencies, but normally this applies only under limited stimulus conditions. For example, we seldom, if ever, make swimming motions on land, nor are we tempted to make golf swings without a club in our hands. These behaviours may have been well acquired on the basis of reinforcement, but this acquisition process has occurred under specific stimulus conditions. The organism which has been conditioned learns not only the appropriate response, i.e. the one that is reinforced, but also the specific situation or the discriminative stimuli in the presence of which that response is reinforced. Making swimming motions on land is seldom reinforced; making them in water is reinforced. These silly examples introduce a point of fundamental importance. Learning the appropriate discriminative stimuli under which a particular response will be reinforced is a cardinal issue in all social behaviours and, more relevantly, is an essential component of all sport. If an opponent produces a bit of behaviour, a top-spin serve for example, the appropriate response will be made by the other player, and hence receive reinforcement, only if he has learned to associate that particular discriminative stimulus (a way of holding the racket or alteration of the swing) with that response. Examples of this kind are legion in all sports and we do not need to expand them here. What is important at this point is to grasp the significance of the fact that responses are brought under the control of discriminative stimuli when only these responses are reinforced in their presence and are not reinforced in the presence of any other stimuli.

Stimulus control is an obvious characteristic of behaviour, but what is less obvious is the fact that any response which has been learned in the context of one discriminative stimulus has *thereby* been learned as a response in the presence of other similar stimuli. This phenomenon is known as stimulus generalization and both laboratory and real-life examples are easily described. If a rat has learned that pressing a lever is reinforced only in the presence of a tone of given frequency and not at any other time, we can describe the tone as a discriminative stimulus and will observe that the rat reserves its lever pressing behaviour for those times when the tone is sounded. If we now change the frequency of the tone, the rat will still respond. We speak of generalization having occurred. In terms of skilled behaviour, we can observe the same process. To use our previous example, the tennis player may never have played his opponent before and hence have never seen the particular stimulus of this player producing a top-spin serve before. Yet he may produce the appropriate response the first time he is faced with the situation. The new stimulus conditions also produce the appropriate behaviour. One of the central aspects of this phenomenon is that the probability with which a response will occur in the presence of the new stimulus is highly dependent on the similarity between the new stimulus and the stimulus under which the response was previously reinforced. In other words, if a new stimulus differs markedly from the original, the response will not occur. Where it is possible to grade a response in terms of its strength, we find a gradual reduction in strength as the new stimulus becomes increasingly different from the original; a generalization gradient. From this point it is a simple matter to deduce that the range of generalization is very flexible depending upon the consequences of the process. In our example, generalization was useful since it enabled an appropriate response to occur in the presence of the new stimulus. That response is likely to be reinforced and so the process of generalization is reinforced. On the other hand, generalization may be inappropriate in many circumstances and the response may not receive reinforcement and hence become extinguished. For example, a soccer player may see a particular body movement on the part of an opponent. In the past, a response of moving to the right may have been reinforced by an interception when a similar stimulus was presented. In performing this response he may fail to be reinforced because the opponent goes in the opposite direction. His generalization results in his being beaten. If this occurs on more than one occasion with that opponent, the extinction process will occur and alternative responses perhaps receive reinforcement. Essentially, therefore, generalization and discrimination become two interlocking processes. An organism is reinforced for generalizing a response in the presence of some similar stimuli and is reinforced for discriminating between other similar stimuli. This is a point to which we shall return, but it is perhaps obvious that much of our skill learning involves these discriminative and generalizing processes.

One phenomenon associated with recent investigations into discrimination training has become known as the behavioural contrast effect. If an organism is reinforced for responding in the presence of two distinct stimuli, response rates in the presence of both stimuli tend to be equivalent. If these stimuli are available alternately in the experimental situation, there is no discrimination in terms of responding. When responding has become firmly established discontinuation of the reinforcement for responding in the presence of one stimulus leads to the extinction of the response in the presence of that stimulus. The interesting aspect of this procedure is that responding in the presence of the other stimulus markedly increases. No change in reinforcement in the presence of that stimulus occurs but the frequency of responding increases dramatically. Introducing discriminative properties for a cue may therefore have a considerable influence on performance even though the contingencies of reinforcement remain unchanged.

It is perhaps less obvious, but it is also true that response generalization occurs during the acquisition of a particular response. In the abstract, we can say that when a response has been learned to a particular stimulus, other similar responses have also been learned in the process. If one response has been acquired as a result of reinforcement, other similar responses are also likely to occur. In other words, a stereotyped response may be produced by the animal and be reinforced, but variations on that behaviour have also been acquired. In one sense this is the fundamental basis of the shaping of behaviour. When we shape a behaviour, we reinforce a response which approximates the desired behaviour and then await a variation on that response which more closely resembles our objective. This behaviour is then reinforced and so on, until the behavioural goal is achieved.

Reciprocal and multiple reinforcement
In operant conditioning texts it is conventional to treat the concept of reinforcement in its implications for a single organism. We have said, for example, that praise as a secondary reinforcer, can be used to maintain or manipulate and modify a bit of behaviour. The implication that we have not discussed is the fact that this means two people are interacting together. Reinforcement is a two-way process. We can think for example, in terms of a coach and a player. The player's behaviour has been modified or may be changed by the coach's use of reinforcement, but what maintains the coach's behaviour? Presumably the fact that either the situation or the player is reinforcing his coaching behaviour is important. A coach may be reinforced because his particular strategy of coaching produces winners for which he receives either money or prestige or some other form of reinforcement. It is just as legitimate to view the experimenter as being reinforced by his animals as it is to view the animals as being reinforced by the experimenter. The experimenting behaviour only continues provided it is reinforced. In understanding complex human behaviour in which people interact with one another it is essential to remember this dual, two-way process of reinforcement.

In the study of animal behaviour in the laboratory, the control exerted over the organism's environment enables us to draw very definite conclusions about the influence of one particular reinforcement on a single response. This capacity is greatly reduced in the examination of real-world human behaviour. One of the significant reasons for this is the fact that human behaviour may be under the control of many different reinforcing agencies. A child may be reinforced for one set of behaviours by his parents and yet find that the same behaviour is not reinforced or is punished by his peer group. This division between reinforcing agencies makes prediction of behaviour far more difficult in real-life than would be suggested by an outline of the deterministic Skinnerian viewpoint. The problem is further complicated by the fact that there are not only competing reinforcement contingencies operating at a given point in time, but there are also likely to exist temporal variations in reinforcement. A behaviour may receive short-term reinforcement, but long term punishment or vice versa. Let us suppose, for example, that the short-term consequence of distance running is an unpleasant physical state; sweating, difficulty in breathing, aching legs, etc. These are aversive stimuli which follow that particular response. In other words, the response of distance running is punished. The long term effects, however, may be very reinforcing. An increase in positive health is an example of a potential long-term reinforcement or Olympic gold medals and prestige. As we shall see later this is an over-simplification of a complex situation, since there is likely to be a temporal continuum of reinforcement, but the example illustrates the point that short and long term consequences of a particular behaviour may be completely different.

Some Major Findings

When we apply an operant conditioning procedure to an organism, the initial shaping process may take some considerable time to achieve. The length of time will depend on the nature of the response to be achieved and the organism we are using. After the desired response has first been made, there is a fairly consistent pattern to the acquisition process. The operant behaviour appears with increasing frequency and other non-reinforced behaviours are eliminated. The position is eventually reached where, when the appropriate stimulus is presented, only the operant behaviour occurs. It is usual to find that the acquisition curve is negatively accelerated. For each addition of unit conditioning time, the increment in response strength is smaller. There are relatively large increases in frequency at first and increases become progressively smaller until eventually an asymptote is reached. The asymptote is a stable level of responding and represents the maximal rate for that response under the conditions obtaining.

Although this generalization concerning rate of acquisition is defensible, it is only a generalization. The negatively accelerated curve is often an artifact of averaging the results of many subjects. A single reinforcement may have considerable impact on the frequency of a response for a given organism. For this reason, much operant conditioning research is reported by showing the performance of an individual organism rather than average results.

It should be noted that the measures of performance cited here are typical in experimental operant conditioning. Most often the measure used is the frequency of a response which the organism can freely make within the experimental situation, for example, a rat pressing a lever or a pigeon pecking a key. Negatively accelerated acquisition curves are just as typical in more constrained situations. If the required response of a rat is alleyway running, the experimenter has control of the frequency of responding. However, if speed is used as the measure of response strength, an identical average development of the response occurs.

The most efficient way of reaching the asymptote is by the reinforcement of the response each time it is made. Continuous reinforcement is optimum during the acquisition period. If only partial reinforcement is given during this period of time, it is still probable that the response will be acquired, but the process will take longer.

Once the response has become established, continuous reinforcement may no longer be optimum in terms of producing highest levels of response strength. If the reinforced response is a free operant, switching the animal to a partial reinforcement schedule is likely to produce more frequent responding. Where the response is not followed on each and every occasion by its reinforcement, the animal makes a higher number of responses. If such a change is made to a partial reinforcement schedule, a new asymptote will be reached and responding is likely to stabilize at this new higher level. All of the different partial reinforcement schedules mentioned earlier, do not produce the same kind of responding. Responding on a fixed ratio schedule is higher than on continuous reinforcement and shows a remarkable stability. There is a tendency for the animal to pause in its responding after each reinforcement, especially with high ratios of responses to reinforcement. After this pause, responding begins again and is maintained at its steady rate. There is a tendency for a higher rate of responding to be produced the bigger the ratio of responses to reinforcements. There are obviously limits to this tendency, but it is true that if we move from a ratio of 25 : 1 to a ratio of 100 :1, the rate of responding is likely to increase.

When achieving these very high ratios of responding to reinforcement, it is normal for a gradual extension of the response demands to be made. Switching an animal from continuous reinforcement to a schedule of 200 : 1 (demanding 200 responses before reinforcement) would be equivalent to putting the animal on an extinction schedule. However, it is possible to reach very high ratios like this by a process of gradual adjustment. Parenthetically, it is worthwhile pointing out that when animals are working on the highest ratios they may be operating at a net physiological loss. That is, the work output in responding is not compensated for by the quantity of food received in reinforcement. This is additional cause to dispute ascribing intention to the organism with respect to reinforcement. When operating at a net physiological loss, it becomes absurd to think of the organism responding *in order* to get food.

Fixed ratio responding has been likened to piece-work, in which payment is given for a measurable work-output. Fixed interval schedules are more analogous to salaried work. The characteristics of responding under this kind of schedule are quite distinctive. Consequent upon establishing a fixed interval schedule, a stable rate of responding develops. The number of responses made between reinforcements is constant although the distribution of responses within any interval is uneven. There is an initial post-reinforcement pause, similar to that found in fixed ratio, and this is followed by a steadily increasing rate of responding until the next reinforcement is presented. When plotted on a cumulative graph this effect is known as 'scalloping' and is very characteristic of this kind of schedule. If an animal is switched from one fixed interval to another, for example from one reinforcement per thirty seconds to one per sixty seconds, there is a tendency for the same number of responses to be produced in the new interval. That is, the overall rate of responding goes down, but the pattern of the distribution of responses within the interval remains the same.

When the schedules of reinforcement are variable, either variable interval or variable ratio, very high rates of responding are predictable. The greater rates are usually found under the variable ratio schedule, although comparison between the schedules is not entirely legitimate. It is particularly under variable ratio that we find organisms operating at a net physiological loss. Both of the variable schedules produce stable responding. The stability occurs over time and also between reinforcements. Unlike the fixed ratio and fixed interval schedules there are no post-reinforcement pauses.

One indirect measure of response strength, apart from those already mentioned, is the resistance a response shows to extinction. If a response has become well established, termination of the reinforcement results in a greater number of responses occurring before extinction is complete than if the response is less firmly part of the animal's repertoire. The number of responses which follow the termination of reinforcement can therefore be used as an indicator of response strength. When performance has been previously maintained on one of the variable schedules, a greater number of responses tend to occur than after maintenance on the respective fixed schedule. It is also the case that resistance to extinction is greater under partial reinforcement than under continuous reinforcement.

In the application of operant conditioning principles, this finding has both great advantages and disadvantages. If the response is desirable we can rest assured that extinction will not occur, even if there are long periods without reinforcement, after the response has previously been maintained on a variable interval schedule. Should we be attempting to remove an undesirable response, the characteristic of resistance to extinction may make the process very much more difficult. One is never more conscious of this than in the social training of children. Suppose we wish to eradicate a response which we consider has been reinforced in the child by our attention. Failing to attend to the child when he makes the response is the extinction mechanism. Provided we have identified the reinforcement correctly this should lead to the extinction of the response. But two difficulties emerge. Firstly, the process may take a long time if reinforcement has previously been intermittent and secondly, the child may produce the behaviour outside the confines of his own home. In a social setting the parents may be forced to devote attention to the child, effectively restarting the partial reinforcement schedule and making subsequent extinction even more difficult.

In sport, coaches are aware of similar difficulties. Those responses on the part of players which encounter occasional success may not be optimum for performance, but the coach will find extreme difficulty in eradicating them. The partial reinforcement effect will ensure, however, that once the appropriate alternative is acquired, perhaps through counterconditioning, the new response is not easily lost.

The schedule of reinforcement upon which the response has been maintained is one important variable in operant conditioning. Somewhat more obviously, the magnitude of reinforcement also has significant effects upon responding. With two organisms in equivalent states of deprivation, greater response probability will be derived from the organism receiving the larger reinforcement. Frequency of responding, as a measure of response strength, is very sensitive to this variable. We have suggested that response rate is likely to stabilize at some asymptote when other conditions remain constant. If the magnitude of reinforcement per trial is increased, however, there will be a corresponding increase in rate which will in turn stabilize at some new level. The application of progressively larger reinforcements produces diminishing returns. That is, an increment of one unit to a reinforcement of four units will have a much larger effect than an increment of one unit to twenty. This is probably evident from even a cursory glance at real-life reinforcement situations. Thinking in terms of money as reinforcement, an increase of four dollars to five dollars is likely to have a greater influence on response rate than an increase of twenty dollars to twenty-one dollars.

In many experimental situations it is also possible to manipulate the quality of reinforcement while keeping the quantity constant. For example, sweetening of rat food by addition of saccharine is a manipulation of quality which does not change either the nutritional component of the food or the quantity provided. Qualitative changes of this kind do influence response rate, but again the increments are negatively accelerated and a point is eventually reached where no further increment in response rate is achieved by an increase along the qualitative dimension.

The qualitative differences are even more noticeable in man. A coach, as reinforcing agent, may provide praise to reward a player. The quantitative dimensions of this stimulus are closely allied to qualitative aspects. Throughout our lives we have had practice in detecting subtle differences in the verbal behaviour of others. The quality of the reinforcement will be determined by the nuances of intonation and associated facial expressions as much as by the nature of the words themselves. Sarcasm or irony may completely change a given verbal comment from reinforcement to punishment.

It has become an axiom of operant conditioning that immediate reinforcement produces faster acquisition of responses. Any delay of reinforcement after the response has occurred is likely to make acquisition less efficient. For one thing, the animal may engage in other behaviours which are not desired during the interval and it may be these which receive the reinforcement and hence increase in frequency. Delays in the presentation of primary reinforcement may be mediated, however, by the use of secondary reinforcers. For example, an animal may receive a token which has developed secondary reinforcing characteristics and not receive his primary reinforcement for a considerable period. In man the capacity to tolerate long delays in reinforcement and yet still find reinforcement having its effect is much greater than in other organisms.

Part of the impact of Skinner's *Beyond Freedom and Dignity* lies in the identification of our society as having chosen punishment as its major method of control. In legal systems, religious systems, education, government and in social interactions there are mechanisms of sanctions for use against those who flout the rules. Without overemphasizing the point western culture has rightly been called a punitive society.

What are the effects of punishment? The laboratory investigation of punishment has established some important facts about the process, many of which are surprising to the lay man. Punishment can stop the animal making the response, as we should predict, but this only happens in very limited situations. For example, if high intensity punishment is used, the undesired response may be quickly eliminated. When the punishment is of a relatively low intensity, responding may not be changed at all. The intermediate ranges of punishment produce the most interesting effects. It has been found that if a previously reinforced response is punished with medium severity the result is a reduction in the occurrence of the behaviour. However, this reduction is only temporary and the punishment is only effective so long as it continues to be presented. It is not true to say that the response is eliminated, because after punishment is terminated the response may reappear. In fact in some studies it has been shown that after punishment was stopped the response actually increased in frequency to a level greater than that being produced before punishment was initiated. It has become typical to refer to this phenomenon as the suppression of behaviour through the use of punishment. The effect is most clearly observed if an animal is given variations of punishment in alternating experimental sessions. As the intensity of punishment is changed the rate of responding changes accordingly. Moderate punishment produces some suppression, intense punishment almost total suppression and when this is changed to no punishment, response rate begins to climb again and so the cycle may be repeated.

Two additional aspects of punishment need to be discussed. The relationship between the behavioural effects of the punishment and the response is important in determining the effectiveness of the punishment in terminating undesirable behaviour. If a rat has been trained to run an alleyway on the basis of positive reinforcement, electric shock through a grid floor may be regarded as an effective punishment which should at least suppress the behaviour. But if the shock is delivered to the back legs of the animal the result is faster running. The same punishing stimulus may result in the facilitation of the undesired response rather than its elimination. In everyday terms, smacking a child for crying is unlikely to be effective in eliminating that behaviour.

The other point is that punishing is likely to result in other behaviours which may in themselves be undesirable. If an organism has come to associate punishment with a particular situation, there are likely to occur attempts at escape from that situation or future avoidance of the situation. Just as positively reinforced behaviour is said to come under stimulus control, so stimuli associated with the presentation of punishment may come to elicit avoidance or escape responses. There is also a probability that punishment may be associated with emotional responses such as anxiety, fear or hate which may interfere with the production of other responses which we are trying to condition. Notice that this emotional effect may also occur if negative reinforcement is used. Even though the organism is rewarded by its termination, the aversive stimulus may still be associated with undesirable emotional effects.

This is one situation in which there is a combined effect of respondent and operant conditioning. The punishing stimulus may reflexively elicit responses. If these are not compatible with the operant the punishment will be very effective. The stimuli associated with the operant will come to elicit the new conditioned respondent. Where there is some compatibility between the respondent and the operant the punishing stimulus may be less effective. This is the case in which running on the part of the rat is punished by shock to the back legs. The shock is likely to elicit a forward jump which is not incompatible with the operant of running.

When a person such as a coach uses verbal or other forms of punishment, it must also be remembered that he himself is a stimulus present during the process. Those avoidance responses which are likely to be developed to the aversive stimulus may become conditioned to this stimulus. In other words, the coach or physical education teacher may become a cue for the initiation of avoidance responses. Even if this does not appear overtly in the individual, it may serve to reduce the effectiveness of the coach as future dispenser of positive reinforcement.

Punishment loses its effectiveness very rapidly when there is an interval of time between the production of the response and its administration. If punishment is to be effective, even in suppressing behaviour, it is essential that it is presented immediately after the response occurs. Just as reinforcement will lose its effectiveness if delay is introduced, so is punishment likely to decrease in efficiency.

Considering these facts concerning punishment, it is superficially surprising that our society should have selected this method of control as a prime means of modifying behaviour. If we bear in mind the reciprocal relationship between the controller and the controlled, the reason becomes obvious. Since the administration of punishment produces short-term suppression of responses, the punisher receives immediate reinforcement for his use of punishment. In other words he is rewarded for punishing by having the behaviour terminated at least temporarily. When the situation occurs again the punisher is more likely to use this method since it received reinforcement in the past. Skinner remarks at one point that, 'People quickly become skilful punishers (if not, thereby, skilful controllers), whereas alternative positive measures are not easily learned. The need for punishment seems to have the support of history, and alternative practices threaten the cherished values of freedom and dignity.'

Summary
Armed with these basic principles of behaviour it is possible to consider the phenomenon of sport within society in its various aspects. The first task is to examine the different facets of sport and describe what currently exists in terms of these principles. Having achieved a description of sport it might then be possible to go on to consider how changes in the situation may be brought about.

Section Two   Determinants of Sports Behaviour

Introduction
Sport includes many diverse forms of behaviour, from highly cerebral games of strategy to the application of maximal force in a single response. The definition of sport and the classification of activities as sport or not sport need not concern us here. Much of our analysis is abstract and could be applied to any of the activities which come under the umbrella term.

The major task in this section is the examination of the reinforcements available for participation in sport. This section seeks to give a behavioural answer to the question, 'why does man participate in sports?' There have been a number of previous answers to this question. The majority have involved reference to autonomous man. A 'play instinct' has been cited as a reason for participation, a competitive human nature has been blamed and others have used explanations in terms of drives to fulfil our physical potential. These accounts, and many variations of them, appear to explain the behaviour by referring us to internal and unknowable causes. In other words they simply avoid the question and explain nothing. It is argued in this section that such mentalistic explanations are unnecessary and it is possible to explain sports participation using only those principles and related evidence which were outlined in the last section. Not only can we find the reasons for participation in these principles, but they also provide an answer to the question 'why do many people fail to participate in sport?' This problem has been posed much less frequently and is often unanswerable when participation has been explained on the basis of human nature or play instincts. The third section deals with this problem in detail.

Participation
In a Skinnerian analysis, the problem of participation is both simple and highly complex, depending on our approach. If we consider the problem of participation on the basis of an individual, the answer is very straightfoward. We must simply direct our attention to the individual's history of reinforcement. His behaviour has been shaped by the environment in which he has developed. This environment has provided him with reinforcements for some behaviours and not for others. Where the individual participates in sport, we conclude that either this behaviour has been reinforced in the past and is now gradually undergoing extinction or the behaviour is still receiving some kind of reinforcement.

This explanation is very straightforward and describes the way in which a behaviour is produced and maintained and answers the question why. The question becomes more complicated if we now ask 'why do cultures provide reinforcement for sport?' In order to answer this question, we need to examine what we mean by a culture. Skinner (1971) reexamined the anthropological definition of culture. Instead of suggesting that a culture '. . .consists of traditional ideas and their attached values,' Skinner made the following analysis:

> But those who observe cultures do not see ideas or values. They see how people live, how they raise their children, how they gather or cultivate food, what kinds of dwellings they live in, what they wear, what games they play, how they treat each other, how they govern themselves, and so on. These are the customs, the customary *behaviours,* of a people. To explain them we must turn to the contingencies which generate them. . . . The social contingencies, or the behaviours they generate, are the 'ideas' of a culture; the reinforcers that appear in the contingencies are its values. (Skinner, 1971).

Within much of western culture sport receives reinforcement. Our culture has the 'idea' that sport is 'good'. We can reword this statement in Skinnerian terms in the following way: sporting behaviour is generated by social contingencies of positive reinforcement within our culutre. The idea and the value are included within the statement.

Any individual within a culture is subject to the social contingencies of that culture. But the culture may also reinforce him for maintaining the social contingencies of that culture. In other words, he may have acquired the tendency to reinforce in others those behaviours for which he has been reinforced. Skinner points out that in this way a culture becomes self-perpetuating. A specific aspect of behaviour may develop in a culture as a response to particular physical or social changes. This may be transmitted to future generations and the behaviour still occur even when the original reason has long since disappeared. These considerations are entirely relevant to the question of participation in sport within our society. There may have been conditions in the past in which the behaviour developed and received reinforcement. Those conditions may now have passed but the behaviour is maintained, since its contingencies are transmitted from generation to generation. The individual is both conditioner and conditioned.

A phenomenon of behaviour as diverse as sport cannot be explained in terms of a single causal set of situations within a culture, but we may use two or three examples to clarify these issues. A link has often been made between the development of sport and militarism. When threatened from outside, a culture may have found that aggressive responses have been reinforced in the past. In order to make such responses a culture needs strong and healthy males. By providing reinforcements for sport a culture may believe it is going some way towards achieving this. This has been the case in many crises and wars. It should be pointed out, however, that seldom do cultures operate with a clear

26

understanding of principles of behaviour. Therefore, the reinforcement contingencies used to produce a population of fit males have seldom been planned efficiently. In times of war a government may simply exhort its population to be 'fit for the struggle' and claim that physical training is patriotic. The effectiveness of this move depends then upon the degree to which behaving patriotically is reinforced socially within that culture. If an individual begins training and receives social approval and esteem, the result may be increased physical fitness within the nation. Because governments tend to use positive reinforcement inefficiently they may even find that they only receive the reinforcement consequent upon a fit population by using aversive techniques with their population. They may issue orders concerning training and develop punishment systems for failure to comply.

Our point in this regard is that by whatever means, and for whatever reason, sporting behaviour becomes a part of a behavioural complex within a culture, that behaviour will persist if the population continues to maintain the appropriate social reinforcement contingencies. If an individual receives reinforcement for participating in sport and is also reinforced for reinforcing the participation of others, the phenomenon is likely to persist even though the original reason for reinforcement is no longer a factor. The increase in participation may continue even though the threat of war is no longer present.

Although many of the reasons for participation in sport and its reinforcement by cultures may be of historical interest only, there are current governmental reinforcements for participation which demand some explanation. Sport is now international and competition between nations is very common. Success in international competition is reinforced at an international level. The prestige awarded to a nation or culture may be so reinforcing that. it in turn reinforces participation within the nation. By demonstrating supremacy at an international level, a nation may achieve status in the eyes of others and this status may lead that nation to reinforce sports behaviour. This has been the case, particularly, where nations behave as though any demonstration that those living in one political system are better in some way than those in another is a reflection of the quality of the system as a whole.

A government, as a controlling agency within a culture, also obtains reinforcement from the members of that nation. This has been called the counter-control system. In most western cultures the counter-control mechanisms are quite effective. A government may therefore be punished (voted out of power) or reinforced (reelected or granted public approval) for its actions. If a government provides reinforcement for sport and in return receives reinforcement from its own population, this behaviour is likely to continue. In this way, governments act as controlling agents only to the extent that they are allowed to control. We must also remember that governments are made up of people whose behaviour is also the product of the social contingencies of reinforcement and punishment within that culture. The fact that governments do reinforce sport should not therefore be surprising.

What reinforcements are governments capable of supplying for sporting behaviour? This may be accomplished in a number of ways. The reinforcement may be provided in terms of money for sports. This may take many different forms, from the provision of facilities to the payment of national coaches, from the financing of national teams to the allocation of lottery funds to sports promoters. These payments may reinforce directly or indirectly. For example, payments to organizers of sports do not increase participation directly. However, if the continuation of support is contingent upon increased participation or increased quality of performance, then the organizer produces, in turn, those behaviours which reinforce participation by others.

Money is not the only reinforcer which governments apply. They may use techniques of granting prestige and esteem to those who have achieved success. The regular appearance of sportsmen in Honours lists is an example of this and many nations employ similar systems, with badges, diplomas, government sinecures and other less tangible reinforcers applied to sports behaviour.

As we have pointed out, governments do not generally base their application of reinforcement in any coherent way. They will frequently use low strength reinforcers which are of little value in changing behaviour.

The degree to which cultures reinforce sport through their governments is variable. We must not lose sight of the fact that although most western cultures place a positive 'value' on sport, this is a recent phenomenon in many cultures and is still by no means universal. Punishment has been used against sports behaviour of various kinds in many countries and is not regarded as an area of governmental concern in many others.

Not only are there existing cultural differences in the degree to which sport is reinforced, but there are also significant differences in the kinds of sport which are reinforced. Again, many of these variations may have historical bases, however there are also physical characteristics which play an important role in determining which sports a culture will reinforce. Climatic differences are an obvious example. Winter sports cannot be reinforced if there is not at least reasonably easy access to snow and ice and, conversely, a sport such as swimming might be difficult to reinforce in the same location that provides opportunity for skiing. The geography of a country may also have an impact. It should not be surprising that the Netherlands provides more reinforcement for cycling than Switzerland.

The extent to which a nation provides reinforcement for sport depends upon the degree to which that nation derives reinforcement itself for its reinforcing behaviour. However, nations may also differ in the extent to which they are capable of reinforcing. If we simplify the situation by examining only reinforcement through money, the point becomes clear. Whereas the developed nations can afford to spend money in reinforcing participation in sport, those less wealthy may not consider this a worthwhile use of funds. The returns in reinforcement for the nation may not be sufficient. Skinner often refers to this as 'good husbandry' with respect to available reinforcers. We attempt to maximize the use of the reinforcers we have available. In this sense, governments may apply reinforcers to those behaviours of the population which, in turn, will give the maximum amount of reinforcement. For example, the United States receives credit and prestige from many activities. It also has the finances available to reinforce sport and therefore achieve yet more prestige. A small backward country with very limited resources may find that sport is one way in which prestige is achieved and therefore spend money in that direction. In other words, it is not merely a question of a surplus of money which is important in determining whether a nation reinforces sport, but an interaction between the amount of reinforcement derived by the nation in terms of prestige and the availability of reinforcing potential within the country.

Professionalism

Cultures have seen fit to reinforce sport or punish it or ignore it. The governmental impact on participation in sport may be likened to the top stratum in a hierarchy of reinforcements for sport. Somewhat below this level, since obviously influenced by legislation, comes the currently important commercial reinforcement of sport. Vast sums of money are available to supreme athletes and professionalism has developed in many of the lower levels of sports. The growth of professionalism is an illustration of the awareness of the potency of money as a secondary and generalized reinforcer. If we wish to maintain a behaviour and increase its strength of occurence we choose the most effective reinforcer. In the past, such reinforcers as prestige and status may have been used. However, these were apparently insufficient in the pursuit of behavioural goals and hence stronger and more satisfying reinforcers have been used. The historical shift from amateurism to professionalism in sport may be viewed in these terms. The word professional was used derogatively during the last and for a large proportion of this century. The reinforcements derived from status, prestige and some inherent aspects of the sport (the love of the sport) were deemed sufficient. Whenever efficiency of the behaviour becomes of increasing importance, as with the growth of international competition, these reinforcers may become inadequate and the alternative and stronger reinforcer of money has to be substituted.

In a sense this transition has been brought about by an unspoken acceptance of behavioural determinism. Credit or prestige would be given to the man for his performance as though this were a reflection of some inner supremacy of his which accounted for his winning. The role of his history of training or participation in the sport was disregarded as detracting from this inner quality. Thus, people who obviously trained themselves or received money for training themselves could not be accredited with this inner supremacy and hence were somewhat frowned upon. When it became impossible to ignore the causal relationship between training and performance (since those who trained did all the winning) the concept of inner supremacy fell by the wayside. From that point we can trace a gradual search for appropriate reinforcements. This has taken many forms, but the most significant change in this context has been the enormous increase in sums of money paid to sportsmen. Skinner explains this in terms of other professions in the following way: 'members of the leisure classes have generally lost status when they submitted to pecuniary reinforcement by "going into trade." . . . The loss in status may explain why most professions have come only slowly under economic control.'

In sport the trend is still continuing. The strength of money as a positive reinforcer for sport made its appearance in the last century and further inroads have been made recently. The removal of the distinction between 'gentlemen' and 'professionals' in cricket is one example of this, but recent changes in tennis are also symptomatic. Perhaps the Olympic Games are the final official adherent to the doctrine of amateurism at an international level and the degree to which this is an adherence to the original code is extremely variable between countries.

At the present time commercial interests appear superficially to dominate the reinforcement structure within sport. The professional sportsmen are the ones who capture headlines and receive national and international attention. These sportsmen are merely the tip of the iceberg and represent only a small proportion of those who participate in sport. Although participation in sport is maintained and strengthened on the basis of monetary reinforcement, this source of reinforcement is not adequate to explain either the massive popular participation in sport nor the acquisition of sporting behaviour. People do not begin their participation in sports as professionals.

The use of money as a reinforcer in sport is an interesting phenomenon for the behavioural scientist. Money is manipulated in terms of quantity and the quality of responding in the sporting behaviour is the basis for increments of reward. Unlike the laboratory situation, however, the schedule of reinforcement follows an opposite path. In the laboratory the acquisition of behaviour is produced on the basis of continuous reinforcement and the schedule is then usually changed to some partial system of reinforcement. In terms of monetary reinforcements for sport the reverse is usually the case. The sportsman will receive only occasional or no reinforcement in the form of money during the acquisition period. Having proved his adequacy in the behaviour, he may become professional and receive what would be analogous to continuous reinforcement. This reversal of laboratory strategy can be explained in terms of other reinforcement systems. For example, the behaviour is acquired on the basis of social approval or esteem and praise used as reinforcements which are effectively the initial reason for the occurrence of the behaviour. It is only at later stages that this is supplemented by the additional reinforcement of money.

On the basis of the laboratory studies there is a prediction which could be made concerning the extinction of responding. Partial reinforcement of a response produces greater resistance to extinction than continuous reinforcement. The prediction would, therefore, be that when a professional ceases to be paid for his responding, sports behaviour should terminate more quickly than that of the amateur whose behaviour has been only partially reinforced, perhaps through winning. In other words, after the amateur has ceased gaining his sporadic reinforcement he should continue to participate for a longer period of time. Whether there exists empirical evidence for this I don't know, but a survey of retired sportsmen might provide interesting information. Since the behaviour is multiply reinforced through many different means, each of which could continue after the end of financial reward, we might not expect a clear cut distinction, but in terms of statistical probability, it is a legitimate prediction to make on the basis of laboratory evidence.

An additional distinction between traditional laboratory findings and the payment of athletes may be observed in the rate of responding. Under a partial reinforcement schedule we typically find higher rates of responding relative to performance under continuous reinforcement schedules. When we speak of the professional sportsman receiving continuous reinforcement and yet certainly spending more time at his sport than a partially reinforced amateur, we are faced with an apparent contradiction. However, the contradiction is easily explained. The comparison between schedules is made in the laboratory in terms of the single response under observation. In real-life situations reinforcements compete in their influence upon total behaviour patterns. Thus, the amateur is receiving continuous reinforcement in monetary terms from his regular work. This responding is a competing response tendency which is well established. The specific operant (sports behaviour) under consideration may be produced with maximal frequency outside the constraints of the competing reinforcement of gainful employment. The comparison between the rate of responding or number of responses between an amateur and a professional is like comparing the number of responses made by a rat with continuous reinforcement kept unremmitingly in the experimental environment and a rat which is on a partial reinforcement schedule while in the experimental environment, but is frequently returned to a home cage where it receives continuous reinforcement for a totally different response.   An additional distinction must be made between laboratory performance and the real-life situation. When a rat is responding on any schedule of reinforcement it is unusual to find any other contingency placed on its behaviour. In real life this is not the case. The professional sportsman receives continuous reinforcement for his behaviour, but is also under the threat of removal of that reinforcement if he does not comply with some authority. He may be dismissed if he fails to train, for example. This additional factor may make for higher-level responding than would be predicted on the basis of continuous reinforcement alone.

A similar point can be made with respect to the schedule of reinforcement. As we have seen, there is a tendency for a post-reinforcement pause in responding when an organism is reinforced on a fixed interval basis. If a player is paid a good salary, this is analogous to a fixed interval schedule, but there may be little post-reinforcement pause if aversive consequences follow a break in responding. A manager or coach may threaten that failure to report for training will result in the termination of a contract.

The value of a reinforcement is highly dependent on an organism's state of deprivation. Our prediction for sport should be that professional sport would be a behaviour selected with higher probability by those from lower income groups. Within these groups there is a greater likelihood that money will be an effective reinforcer, hence produce greater chance of accepting professional status. Again the question of alternative and competing reinforcements is important. Where a number of well-paid jobs are equally available selection of one may be unpredictable in the sense that it will depend on the history of reinforcement experienced by the individual in all its complexity. The sportsman from the middle classes may be in the situation of being able to receive comparable reinforcement to that obtained in sport through a number of different avenues. The sportsman from the lower class may find the reinforcement from sport to be greater than any of the competing alternatives.

I think, without figures available, that an examination of participation in professional sport would bear out this prediction. It is certainly true historically, that the rise of professional sport in England stemmed from the working class and industrial areas and that professional sport was limited to these areas for a number of years. Similarly, the domination of professional sport by under-privileged groups is perhaps symptomatic of the same issue. If one wished to examine the phenomenon in lay terms it is possible to view professional sport as a way out of the ghetto when alternatives are relatively few and far between. The description of boxers as being 'hungry' or not sums up the distinction I am trying to make. The particular brand of responding reinforced in the sport of boxing makes this apposite, but it would be just as accurate to refer to a 'hungry' footballer or 'hungry' baseball player. We simply mean that the relative magnitude of the reinforcement for these people is much greater than for others.

It is in observations of this kind where the concept of motivation may be usefully applied. In this context we are dealing with unequal states of deprivation and resulting behaviour patterns. The reinforcement of a given amount of money will have greater influence on behaviour if there is a greater deprivation of money.

The growth in salaries of professional sportsmen to the present has been a significant aspect of sport. One is tempted to regard this as a factor related to the foregoing conclusions. As the pursuit of excellence has gained momentum there has been a demand that all who are capable of superior performance should be participants. The obvious way to achieve maximal participation is to offer reinforcements greater than competing alternatives. The student leaving University, for example, is faced with a choice of behaviours. When one option is participation in a sport this behaviour may well be chosen because of the high levels of reinforcement offered through contracts in present-day professional sport. A number of years ago an alternative may have been just as attractive. In other words, there is perhaps a reducing tendency for class distinctions in professional sports. Current high levels of reinforcement may make the selection of this behaviour more probable for a greater cross-section of society.

Spectating

In order to round out a discussion of professional sports one needs to explain why the behaviour is reinforced. Why are sports promoters so anxious to disburse large reinforcements? Again the answer lies in the reinforcement they receive in monetary terms. Promoting, as a behaviour, is reinforced by money from fans, amongst other things, and promoting is terminated rather quickly when this reinforcement ceases. If we carry on the analysis one stage further and ask what is the reinforcement for fanatical behaviour, the question becomes very complex. Spectating, as an aspect of behaviour for which people are prepared to trade in secondary reinforcers (money), is so common and such a basic element of professional sport that it demands an explanation. Why do people spectate at sporting events? What reinforcers have, in their past, led to this bit of behaviour becoming an important part of their repertoire of responses?

The popularity of spectating as a pastime indicates that reinforcements must be particularly powerful. One can speculate that there is likely to be a diversity of reinforcement which results in this behaviour. Not everyone in a soccer stadium is there for the same reason. Firstly, one can observe that big-time professional sport is a spectacle which, in the context of most people's everyday experience, is both novel and intensely stimulating. It is well known from laboratory studies that when organisms are deprived of sensory stimulation they will learn and maintain responses on the basis of stimulation as reinforcement. Research with monkeys in closed environments has demonstrated that a response such as lever pressing can be conditioned if the equivalent of spectating behaviour is used as reinforcement. The system works like this. A monkey is placed in a closed and rather dimly illuminated cubicle which contains a lever. The desired response is lever pressing. If we are using a continuous reinforcement schedule, every time the lever is pressed, a window in the cubicle flips open and allows the monkey to look out into the rest of the experimental area with all its on-going activity for a short time. This is sufficient reinforcement for that response to be well conditioned.

The analogy with spectating is, I think, very close indeed. The urban dweller of today is not exactly locked into his cubicle, but is certainly fed on a relatively unchanging diet of sensory stimulation. Alternatives to this are probably reinforcing. The stimulation provided by the game, the crowds of people around, the shouting, cheering, etc., is probably a fundamental aspect of the reinforcement of spectatorship. The fact that individuals still go to live performances when they could equally well, in some cases, watch the game in greater comfort and with the benefit of replays, at home on their television, seems to indicate that the stimulation provided by the situation has an important influence on this behaviour.

Beyond this general observation, it is probable that spectating depends on highly idiosyncratic reinforcements. The author remembers being told on first trying a North American hot dog, that he hadn't really tasted a hot dog until he had eaten one on a hot afternoon watching a baseball game. The reinforcements derived by this gourmet (!) for watching baseball had obviously little to do with the game.

The excitement generated by a game could probably be included under the general heading of stimulation which is reinforcing. But there are other aspects of the game itself which reinforce spectating. For example, there are many who will aver that their reason for spectating is the observation of skill and strategy.

It is from this that they derive the keenest enjoyment. In behavioural jargon we should say that spectating has been reinforced with this enjoyment in the past. (It would not be appropriate to say that they go *in order* to receive this enjoyment since any particular game may be unskilled and a total disappointment—in other words spectating may be punished on any specific occasion.) This appreciation of the expertise of another has been examined very little by behavioural scientists, yet it is an important aspect of human behaviour. In reading novels, looking at pictures, architecture, crafts of all descriptions, we are deriving pleasure from the fruits of someone else's skill. Our reinforcement for our observation comes in the pleasure this gives. Presumably this is a learned emotional response. The relationship between learning and this emotion is difficult to disentangle however. Those who know most about a particular subject are generally those who appear to derive most pleasure from it. Whether the pleasure is a function of the knowledge or the knowledge a product of the pleasure is a moot point. One certainly hears both points of view in subjective impressions. 'I gradually came to appreciate X as I understood it more thoroughly' is heard just as frequently as 'I so enjoyed X that I decided to get to know more about it.' Probably both points of view are accurate and there exists an interaction between learning and pleasure. For whatever reason, it does appear that the appreciation of another's skill is a potent reinforcement for spectating behaviour.

It is a fact of life for promoters of professional sport that spectators increase for winning teams. It would appear therefore, that there is greater reinforcement for watching one's own team win than watching the same team lose. The other reinforcements provided for spectators that we have discussed so far do not account for this difference. The excitement, spectacle and skill (as well as the hot dogs) may be identical and yet the result be entirely different. Winning or losing adds a new aspect of reinforcement. It is perhaps best to examine this phenomenon in the light of our competitive society. Credit is given to those who are successful and those who are not tend to be denigrated. If we feel we are reinforcing behaviour which is not optimum we terminate the reinforcement. By withdrawing our reinforcement for inappropriate behaviours we hope to achieve their modification. When we refuse to reinforce a losing team by paying money in order to watch, we are indicating our disapproval of their behaviour. In other words, the reciprocal relationship of reinforcement is in operation in this situation. We have explained that attendance at professional sport may be reinforced by particular aspects of that sport and at the same time the fans are also reinforcers who will punish or attempt to extinguish certain facets of the sport by withholding their attendance. By failing to attend, fans play the role of controlling agents, whereas in attending their behaviour is under the control of the reinforcement provided by the players. Obviously, this is an over-simplification and it is probable that the two roles of controller and controlled exist with respect to the bit of behaviour (spectating) within the same individual simultaneously.

The role of the crowd as reinforcing agent can be extended to the behaviour while spectating. The boos, whistles and applause are reinforcing to the players for aspects of their behaviour. A participant who 'plays to the gallery' is an indication of how some may be influenced by this. The term is often pejorative and is likely to be used only when the crowd can observe its own impact on that player's behaviour. However, it is likely that all players are affected to some extent by these reinforcers from the crowd. One only needs to ask whether a player prefers to be before a 'home' or an 'away' crowd to find that players certainly feel that they are gaining greater reinforcement (or greater punishment) for their behaviour under these different conditions.

The complication may be extended one stage further. I suggested that fans may fail to support losing teams even when the games are equally exciting and stimulating and skilful. We held these aspects constant while discussing the impact on spectators' behaviour. If a team is beaten regularly and soundly these reinforcers may not remain constant. Excitement may no longer be generated and attendance enter an extinction phase for this reason. The process then becomes a vicious circle. Lower attendance produces lower levels of stimulation and hence less reinforcement for those still attending who may begin to find their attendance extinguishing.

Sports promoters are aware of many of these principles and frequently attempt to produce spectacular additions to the game. Perhaps this has reached its zenith in the half-time show of professional American football. The marching bands, cheer-leaders, parachute landings, movie star appearances all contribute to the game in terms of the diversity of stimulation. The extent to which measurable changes in attendance are produced has not been investigated, but since the promoters continue to receive reinforcement for this activity, the additional spectacle is likely to be preserved even if no causal relationship exists.

A comparison was made earlier between the stimulation derived by physical presence at a game and watching the game on television. Much spectator sport occurs through the medium of television where the reinforcement is much smaller in terms of sensory stimulation. There are certainly many who claim to be bored by a sport on television, but who enjoy the game live. This is surely an indication that there are reinforcers available for watching a live performance rather than on television. One must assume that these reinforcers are the sensory stimuli which are only available at the stadium. The alternative reinforcement of appreciation of skill is probably relatively more important in watching television. One point which needs to be emphasized is that spectating behaviour and its reinforcement is in competition with the reinforcement provided for other behaviours. The fan's wife's nagging may be such an efficient negative reinforcer (one which terminates on the completion of the desired response) that the fan may spend his afternoon mowing the lawn. Other alternative positive reinforcers may also compete effectively and produce different responses or so limit his movement that watching a match on television is a way of optimizing his reinforcement. He can mow the lawn and watch a game on television, but not have time to go to the stadium and back!

Reinforcers for Sport

Within the sporting hierarchy the top class amateur is often as highly revered as the professional and sometimes accorded even greater prestige. The Olympic Games symbolize the pinnacle of amateur sports achievement and gold medal winners may win for themselves status within their country at least equivalent to professional sportsmen. The amateur sportsman of this calibre is often indistinguishable in terms of time devoted to his sport from the professional. The Olympic competitor is likely to spend hours in gruelling training often of great severity. This indicates that the reinforcements for these sportsmen must be extraordinarily powerful. We have just mentioned some of these powerful reinforcers. The prestige and status derived from international level competition can be enormous. This may be sufficient to maintain that behaviour. There are, however, other reinforcements which are just as important. Firstly, in many countries the ethos of the original Olympics has changed beyond recognition. To call many Olympic participants amateurs, is to extend the meaning of that term beyond even its loosest usage. Posts in the army or governmental sinecures are often the reward for 'amateur' accomplishment. The great reinforcer of money in these cases is as much a part of the process maintaining their behaviour as it is for the professional. Added to this there are the additional perks which make high quality amateur performance attractive. Travel to international competitions can be viewed as a reinforcer of great potency. Where these trips are provided through national organizations, they serve to reinforce that severe training which led to them. Foreign travel at the expense of a national sports agency is a reward which may have very great significance, particularly for those who are deprived of foreign travel under every-day circumstances. Associated with the travel are many kinds of subsidiary reinforcers; new people, new views, even the opportunity to escape a particular political system may all serve to act as reinforcers. In a sense this reinforcer could be considered very similar to the stimulation argument which was proposed for the behaviour of fans. A top class amateur is reinforced for his performance by novel and exciting stimulation unavailable to him in his day-to-day existence.

The reinforcers of prestige within society, money and travel are likely to be of greater potency for those who generally lack them than for those who have them available without participation in sport. The prediction can be made on this basis that top-class amateurs are likely to be drawn from those sections of society where these aspects of the environment are lacking. In some respects this is true. Again one can point to the dominance of some minority groups in their country's amateur teams. The American black is a notable example. The status and prestige attached to superior athletic performance may be a much more significant reinforcer for the black underprivileged amateur than for the comparable white. The analysis is confounded somewhat by the demands of the situation. There is still some lip-service paid to the concept of amateurism despite the comments made earlier. The competition between reinforcers then produces complex interactions concerning status and money. While the underprivileged black may find the status a powerful reinforcer, money for some other regular employment may be more powerful. Put in another way, the behaviours which are reinforced in cold cash may oust those which are reinforced with prestige. At least there is a high probability that this will be the case. On the other hand, the middle class white who may be less deprived of status and prestige may be deprived to an even lesser extent of money. He may be supported by a wealthy family or patron and thus find the prestige attached to participation in amateur sports a sufficient reinforcer to maintain his behaviour. The interaction between relative states of deprivation and reinforcers is therefore a significant determinant of the behaviour which is selected from a repertoire.

During this brief description of amateur sport, I have been careful to use the expression 'the maintenance of behaviour'. The reason for this is simple. The reinforcements available to the top class amateur are not available to the novice. It would be inaccurate therefore to think of these powerful reinforcers as producing the acquisition of the behaviour. They merely serve to maintain it once that level of achievement has been reached. They may be supplied to the performer on a variable ratio or a variable interval basis. The prestige not being provided regularly, but on an intermittent basis of course, strengthens the responding. This is the maintenance of a behaviour which has already been acquired and we must look elsewhere for those reinforcements which shaped the acquisition of a particular response.

If we ask the majority of amateurs of low level why they participate in a sport, we are likely to be told that it is simply for enjoyment; for love of the sport. No doubt many professionals and Olympic class amateurs would also give the same answer, so although we have examined some of the potential sources of reinforcement for these groups, no doubt they started out as amateur players and the concept of enjoyment deserves especial consideration. Why are sports so enjoyable that so many people participate in them? What are the reinforcements which produce this behaviour which is often quite meaningless in any utilitarian sense and may sometimes be downright dangerous? Firstly, some of the points we have raised with respect to the upper echelons of the sporting hierarchy can be advanced with respect to the most lowly sporting endeavour. Anyone who has watched a school sports day will note that prestige is awarded to the winners who may have produced the most inferior performances when measured by any outside and objective criterion. Prestige is a relative commodity. To the twelve year old, the status awarded him by his peer group for winning an event at the school sports may be a highly significant reinforcer. This success may reinforce future participation just as the prestige for the Olympic winner may reinforce his continued performance. And this phenomenon of social approval may occur at all levels of performance. The child who is praised and encouraged on a very simple one-to-one basis by a parent or teacher for his first and subsequent efforts is receiving secondary reinforcers which he has come to value and which shape and direct his behaviour.

On a number of occasions we have referred to the reinforcing properties of praise and it is perhaps opportune to discuss verbal behaviour in its role as a controlling agent at this point. In working with animals the use of words is unimportant, but in dealing with complex human behaviours, such as sports, it is essential to realize how much of our social environment consists of the words spoken to us by others. If we wish to extend the behavioural analysis one stage further it is possible to consider thinking as a covert aspect of this verbal environment. Rozynko et al (1973) expressed this point of view in concise form:

> The verbal systems that we possess and share are directly related to our other social behaviours and determine our concept of the world in which we live. A man does much of what he does as a function of what he thinks (or would say) is real. People vote for candidates, go to the theatre, raise their children or build airplanes and sophisticated electronic apparatus as functions of the overt or covert statements about these things that others direct at them. These statements are learned, sometimes paired with autonomic responses (emotions), and are an effect and consequence of the control exerted by verbal communities—the family, the school, the media, religious groups and many other subgroups or institutions. People continue to behave the way they do because of the consequences of their behaviour in the past; similarly, people continue to talk and think the way they do because of the past consequences of their behaviour.

At the simplest level we may modify behaviour by the use of words like 'right' and 'wrong'. We may set a child to participate in sport in this way. By the application of positive verbal statements and the use of verbal reinforcement for similar statements from the child, we also develop verbal responses or covert (thinking) responses which are positive about sport and which may have a significant effect upon participation. In part we are discussing a behavioural analysis of attitudes towards sport and we shall develop this in greater detail later. Because of the extraordinary flexibility of language, it is essential to remember that verbal reinforcers may be extremely subtle and have enormous impact on participation. When a parent verbally reinforces the behaviour of a child he is adding to the total verbal environment, which may have implications beyond the specific skill.

This is often seen with great clarity in educational institutions. Generally speaking one specific kind of behaviour receives reinforcement in this situation. Studying is reinforced in school by the authorities, if not by the peer group. Sports activities give a new dimension to the curriculum in which an alternative group or at least an independent group may be selected for reinforcement. Sport, therefore, represents a special kind of activity in which new people receive reinforcement. Although verbal reinforcement is important this behaviour may be reinforced by the school with prestige, cups, medals and awards in addition to verbal reinforcers which an individual never receives in his academic pursuits. It is easy to explain on this basis the origin of the 'dead from the neck up' stereotype of sportsmen. Deprived of honour and prestige in all other facets of their school work they may be provided with reinforcement by the school authorities for this one kind of activity. Again the relative states of deprivation would cause us to predict that there would be a greater probability of such individuals participating and producing sufficient effort in this different area that they gain success. Although an oversimplification this does form a basis for the myth of the unintelligent sportsman. What is usually forgotten is that the samples of superior school sportsmen and superior school academics are independently based. In other words, superiority is judged on entirely different criteria. In some cases the two may be combined in one individual and sometimes not. We, therefore, tend to forget that there is high prestige for both sport and academic work and if an individual is reinforced for both is likely to produce the behaviours necessary to achieve both.

The observation that social approval is a significant factor in the acquisition of sport may explain some of the emotionally based reasons for participation. It is not by any means comprehensive. Love of a sport or love of sport in general cannot be entirely attributed to this form of reinforcement. There must be alternatives to explain the fact that some people participate in sports when they do not receive social approval for so doing or may even continue to participate in spite of censure. The wife who preferred her husband to mow the lawn rather than spectate at a sport has many counterparts amongst the wives of active sportsmen. Punishment for responding, in technical jargon, or censure for participating in sport in this case, is not a very reliable way of eradicating a response, as we have seen. We should not be surprised that the behaviour continues in spite of this, especially as the behaviour may have been acquired in the past (before marriage?) under conditions of the strong reinforcement of social approval from peer groups or other sources. Even if no source of reinforcement is available, therefore, the extinction process may take a considerable period.

Love of a sport seems to indicate something more positive than the tail end of an extinction process and seems to suggest that there is something *inherently* reinforcing in the sport. No doubt this is the case and it is this inherent reinforcement which is at the core of the phenomenon. There is also little doubt that the precise reinforcements which are affective will vary both from individual to individual and also from sport to sport. Since this appears to be a key to both acquisition and maintenance of sporting behaviour it is worth trying to examine some of the potential reinforcers which come with the sport.

Again we can turn to our monkey in the sealed cubicle for an analogy. Sport of any kind results in stimulation, often intense and often far removed from the humdrum of everyday life. The kind of stimulation may vary enormously: from fishing to rugby football and from golf to motor racing. Notwithstanding these vast differences, the stimulations provided by sports have one thing in common, they differ from the working day stimulation of the participant. The sheer novelty of the stimulation may be the reinforcement which promotes the sporting behaviour. Normally, when we think of the stimulation derived from sport we think in terms of an increment in the intensity of stimulation over everyday life. (This was certainly the point with respect to the reinforcement for spectating.) However, in the examples given above the fallacy of the impression is pointed out. Fishing, as a popular sport, reflects a reduction in the total stimulation over a normal work-level for most of us.

It is a change in stimulation which is important and not so much the direction of that change. There are animal parallels for this contention. Pigeons, for example, who have been kept in a dimly lit cubicle can be trained to perform a particular bit of behaviour when they are reinforced by having the illumination level increased for a period of time. Alternatively, pigeons kept under bright illumination can be reinforced by having the level reduced.

If the environment did not provide a change in stimulation there might be less reinforcement for sports behaviour. Perhaps we should not go as far as Shakespeare in suggesting that 'If all the year were playing holidays, to sport would be as tedious as to work', but the point is made that without the novelty, sport would lose a measure of its reinforcing value.

The change in external stimulation produced through the medium of sport is quite obvious. The bank clerk who rock-climbs at weekends or the salesman who fishes, the engineer who plays cricket, all exchange one physical environment for another. This change serves to reinforce the behaviour. What is also important is the change in internal stimulation. Whenever we move or engage in physical activity we produce internal stimuli. These are internal in the sense that they affect no one else and are our own private sensations produced from muscles, joints and ligaments. This stimulation is just as much a part of the total stimulation which impinges upon us as the external stimuli. By engaging in sport these internal stimuli are changed just as dramatically as the external, perhaps even more so. This change in stimulation may also have reinforcing effects. There is laboratory evidence which supports this contention. If an animal (usually a rat) is kept in restricted quarters which allow it little room for movement, the opportunity to run or work an exercise wheel can be used as reinforcement. A rat will work at pressing a lever if that behaviour results in the opportunity to run. A similar kind of demonstration has been made with children. In this interesting reversal of the usual experimental format, children were reinforced by allowing them to pull levers for eating behaviour. The response of eating was reinforced by allowing movement and activity. The children were not in a state of food-deprivation, but had their eating behaviour manipulated by the reinforcement of self-produced movement. No parent who has admonished a child to finish his supper before going out to play can doubt the validity of movement as a reinforcing agency.

Participation in sport provides opportunity for stimulation of various kinds which reinforce that participation. It is perhaps permissible to translate 'love of sport' into participation due to inherent reinforcers although it is hardly as elegant.

In many cases, the stimulation would not be classified as pleasant on any subjective basis. In fact most observers would label some of the stimulation produced by sport as quite aversive. Skiing may well be punished by a broken leg, boxing by multiple contusions; kicks in the shin, cold, rain and an infinite number of other aversive consequences may follow upon participation in sport. Again we are reminded of the fact that punishment appears to have relatively little impact on responding, especially when the same response has been reinforced over a period of time and is reinforced again after a single punishment. This assumes that those stimuli are classifiable as punishment. Some stimuli associated with sport are extremely difficult to classify in any objective fashion. No one would claim that a broken leg was anything but punishment, but many environmentally produced stimuli are not as obviously punishment or reinforcement. In many sports there is an element of danger, a probability of highly aversive consequences. Let us use the example of rock climbing. Every climber is aware that people are killed and seriously hurt in that sport. The element of danger is paired with the emotional response of fear. Normally, in the laboratory fear is classified as an aversive state. That is, animals will learn those responses which lead to the avoidance of situations which are associated with fear. We can draw a parallel and say that fear may be likened to negative reinforcement. By producing a response the animal terminates the state of fear and hence receives a reward.

Our explanation may stop at this point and we could say that a climber receives his reinforcement through the termination of fear. Skinner makes this point himself. However, it does not explain why the whole business of climbing is not avoided. Rather than avoiding the situation which produces the aversive state the rock climber repeatedly places himself in a situation which results in fear. It seems entirely contradictory that a man should avoid dark alleys in big cities at night, go to great lengths to avoid speaking to a large audience perhaps, ensure that his car is carefully serviced and then spend his weekend searching for a precipitous cliff from which to hang by his nails. The answer to this paradox is that apparently, under controlled circumstances, a state of fear is reinforcing. Frequently we can translate this as the 'thrill' of that sport. Here is a novel and sometimes intense internal sensation which is produced within a specific kind of situation. Although normally aversive, the sensation may be reinforcing. Perhaps the solution to the paradox is embodied in the term 'controlled.' The rock climber has his safety systems worked out and a knowledge of his own skill. The racing driver understands his machine and knows his limitations. The situation, while fear-producing, is under the control of the performer when things are going well. The sensation arising from the situation is then reinforcing. If the situation develops into one outside the control of the performer then the fear so produced may be entirely aversive rather than reinforcing.

One can see in any number of human activities this phenomenon that fear under controlled situations is reinforcing. The manufacturer of fair rides is well aware of it. The majority of rides at a fair provide unusual physical stimulation with a dash of controlled fear and people are prepared to pay for the stimulation this provides.

Inherent in many activities is an improvement in physical well-being. The benefits of regular exercise have long been appreciated and recommended by physicians. The general public appears convinced that 'fitness' may be achieved through sporting activity although there is seldom any definition of the term. Usually the context in which fitness is used suggests that it means a high level of cardiovascular endurance. Regular participation in sports of a vigorous kind is likely to improve cardiovascular endurance and this increased efficiency is a part of positive health. Translating this into a subjective state, we are likely to find that people who participate regularly in sports claim that they feel better for doing so—more healthful, vigorous and virile. No doubt this subjective assessment has its foundation in a changed physiological state but the subjective state, being pleasant, may be reinforcing. Participation in sports is likely to be reinforced because of changes in a subjective feeling of well-being.

One of the problems associated with this reinforcer was mentioned in the first section. It is not delivered immediately after the first response. Changes in cardiovascular endurance, for example, are relatively slow in occurring and require repeated exercise before any positively valued internal change takes place. As we have seen, the acquisition of a response is very much more difficult if it is not reinforced during the early stages. The long term benefits of athletic participation are not derived during the early stages. In fact the long term benefits may be off-set by short term punishment. The neophyte must endure the stiffness, wheezing and soreness accompanying his first efforts in sport. These internal stimuli may be aversive and make future participation in the sport less likely and it may only be at a later stage that the physical aftermath of the activity is sufficiently pleasant as to be reinforcing. There is, therefore, a possibility that long-term and short-term consequences of a sport may be very different. Although an increase in positive health may be important in maintaining the sporting activity, it is of much less value as a reinforcer for the acquisition of the sport.

When short-term consequences are aversive it is superficially surprising that the behaviour is ever acquired at all. The explanation for this is twofold. Firstly, through a gradual exposure to the activity the aversive consequences may be minimized. One does not begin marathon running by attempting twenty-six miles on the first occasion. Tolerance of the discomfort is gradually increased. Secondly, there are likely to be alternative positive reinforcers available which counteract those aversive consequences.

One of these alternative reinforcers may be the social context of the sport. It has been demonstrated repeatedly that membership in a group is a powerful reinforcer for man. It appears that approval of the behaviour of an individual by the group of which he is a member is an important factor in shaping behaviour. One can argue that group norms and attitudes are a reflection of this fact. In order to belong to the group, we have to produce behaviour which is acceptable to them or they are very likely to punish us by exclusion. In our terms, belonging to a group is reinforcement and those behaviours which are reinforced by acceptance in the group are likely to become a part of the individual's repertoire. This phenomenon is most obvious when the behaviour itself is objectionable to other groups. The criminal behaviour of adolescent gangs is an obvious example. One individual from this group may be caught and his parents blame his behaviour on the 'bad influence' of the others. This is saying exactly the same thing in lay terms; that the adolescent did not have criminal behaviour in his repertoire previously, but if he wanted to maintain the acceptance of the gang he had to perform the criminal acts. They reinforced criminal behaviour with acceptance and punished any refusal to perform such acts with exclusion.

In sport, group membership may act as a reinforcer in exactly the same way. Acceptance by the group may be contingent upon participation in the sport. This is probably of greater importance in team sports but may be an aspect of many others too. For many of those involved in team sports the camaraderie of the team and the friendships developed within the context of the sport are extremely important. In maintaining their playing behaviour, the sportsmen gain the reinforcement of this friendship. It is quite possible that in many instances, the friendship would be withdrawn if an individual ceased to participate. It is important that we recognize that the majority of sports, even those which could be labelled as individual rather than team, are indulged in with the company of others. Those fellow sportsmen form a part of the reinforcing contingencies of the environment and serve to maintain that behaviour.

Although it is customary to think of the individual's behaviour being shaped by the group, it should not be overlooked that, as a part of the group, the individual is exerting control over others. The social system which we call a team, for example, consists of individuals who both reinforce behaviours in others which are acceptable to that team and also receive reinforcement when their behaviours are acceptable. Skinner (1953) noted that:

> Selfish behaviour is restrained, and altruism encouraged. But the individual gains from these practices because he is part of the controlling group with respect to every other individual. He may be subject to control, but he engages in similar practices in controlling the behaviour of others. Such a system may reach a 'steady state' in which the individual's advantages and disadvantages strike some sort of balance. In such a state a reasonable control over the selfish behaviour of the individual is matched by the advantages which he gains as a member of a group which controls the same selfish behaviour in others.

It is also true to say that this source of reinforcement may be instrumental in initiating the sports behaviour. Those who are lonely are frequently counselled to 'join a club and make some friends.' In our jargon, the behaviour of going along to the Y.M.C.A. or joining a sports club is reinforced by the social contacts provided within that situation.

Although a sport may be the *raison d'etre* for a club, the sporting behaviour is frequently only a minor component of an elaborate social system. Participation in the sport may be reinforced by different aspects of this social system which have little to do with the sport. The pub is as much a part of rugby as the playing field. The nineteenth is as much a part of golf as the first tee and the après-ski is as much a part of skiing as the down-hill run. In a sense these aspects of the environment of the sport are part of the inherent reinforcers. When individuals speak of their love for a particular sport, these social facets are often as much a part of the object of their affection as the sport itself. For many participants in rugby the opportunity to get drunk with fellow players after a game is the major source of reinforcement. The 'drinking member' of the club is perhaps the epitome and end result of this process. Although those who find their major source of reinforcement in this après-sport social context may be sneered at by those who find their reinforcement provided to a greater extent by other aspects, they are nevertheless the subjects of the same kind of environmental control on their behaviour.

Within many cultures, different sports have been the prerogative of the wealthy. Participants in the sport give a visible indication of their wealth by so-doing. Our culture also provides those people with status and prestige. The result of these culturally determined factors is that even the poorest level of performance in a sport may be reinforced by non-participants with prestige and respect. The general population may reserve its accolades for the superior performer in sports which do not require wealth and at the same time pay respect to the lowliest performer in the status-sports. For example, there was a time when winter holidays were reserved for the very wealthy. By indulging in this activity the performer gained the respect and perhaps envy of his neighbours which was probably highly reinforcing to him. His level of performance on the slopes was irrelevant to the reinforcement. It does not matter that after years of returning to the slopes he had not progressed beyond a snow plough, he received his annual dose of reinforcement from his neighbours for his participation.

There are many other examples of this phenomenon. Sailing, Alpine mountaineering (or better still Himalayan), water skiing, riding, hunting (providing the location is exotic), car rallying, all contain components of this aspect of reinforcement from non-participants which is essentially based on wealth and not quality of performance. The distinction is particularly impressive when we compare the general population's reaction to lower level performances in other sports. The cat-calls and other indignities suffered by the lonely long distance runner in training, change to cheers of support when he becomes an Olympic medallist. The general public punishes his lower level performance and rewards his superior efforts, but the populace seldom jeers the family setting off from home with their new racing dinghy hitched to the car, though they be the poorest of sailors. Perhaps this uncritical respect is simply awarded because the actual performance occurs elsewhere. If the fellows at the office were to contemplate their colleague on his bottom in the snow their respect may be rather more muted.

We have considered many of the reinforcers which are available to the sportsman and perhaps we can attempt to summarize at this point. Money must be regarded as the most significant reinforcer for the upper levels of sporting achievement, but social approval and esteem follow it a close second, whether this comes for only superior performance or for mere participation. Sports provide stimulation either from the activity itself or from the physical and social context in which they take place and this may serve to reinforce the activity. Finally, there are institutions set up around sports which may provide additional reinforcers for participation. It is important to emphasize that these reinforcers overlap and interact with each other. The soccer star may achieve his reinforcement from money, social approval and respect, the stimulation provided by the sport and the fact that all his friends and colleagues are in the game. The interaction is cumulative as progress is made in the sport, which is an interesting departure from the typical laboratory method. The novice may receive few of these reinforcers but as his skill develops the greater rewards are achieved, in greater diversity. This contrasts markedly with the laboratory in which the behaviour is first established on a continuous reinforcement schedule and is then changed to partial reinforcement by which the behaviour may be maintained.

One aspect of the acquisition of sports behaviour which we have not discussed, and may serve as a caution against regarding the behavioural analysis as a total explanation, is the phenomenon of modelling. Experimental work has shown that children will imitate the behaviour of others even when no reinforcement is provided for that behaviour. Children will imitate the observed behaviour of peers and adults and particularly those they hold in high esteem, even when they are on their own and believe, incorrectly, that they are unobserved. Casual observation of children seems to indicate that sports behaviour may be partially acquired through this means rather than strictly through the shaping and reinforcement of behaviour. The first steps towards a sports skill may be the result of viewing the sport on television, for example. However, research evidence shows that in manipulating behaviour, greater changes are brought about by the combination of both reinforcement and modelling and either is less effective on its own. We must conclude from this evidence that an interaction between modelling and reinforcement occurs in the initiation of behaviours which we label as sport.

Although it is usual to contrast imitation and learning through reinforcement, it is not altogether necessary. One could argue that a generalized tendency to imitate is reinforced in children from an early age. Much of the socialization of children consists of reinforcing imitation of specific acts by adults and peers. Any new behaviour which the child observes may not receive direct reinforcement, but the child may produce the behaviour because of the generalized tendency to imitate which has been reinforced in the past. Modelling may be an additional factor in the acquisition of skills, but this does not necessarily remove it from behavioural analysis. During the acquisition of sports skill the relationship between modelling and reinforcement is very close. We may demonstrate and then reinforce the imitation. This will be considered in greater detail in section four.

Section Three   Deterrents to Participation

Introduction

It would appear from the foregoing section that this society provides a great variety of reinforcement for sport. Despite the fact that these reinforcers appear to have led a proportion of the population to participate, they have been unsuccessful in a large number of cases. Why is it that many people go through life abhorring the idea of participation in sport and being bored by watching? Those who actively dislike sport form a sizeable minority of the population, but there are also those who appear simply indifferent to the whole phenomenon. The question a behavioural scientist must try to answer is why are some people influenced by the available reinforcers for sport and why are some people not? To find an answer to this problem it is necessary to review the kinds of individual histories of reinforcement contingencies which potentially lead to non-participation.

On a global scale the most important factor producing non-participation must be the lack of opportunity for sport. Sports are leisure activities which require that basic human needs are first met. When these are not available or when people have to spend a considerable proportion of their time meeting these needs, pursuits which have no material end-product cannot form a significant part of behaviour. To translate this into behavioural terms we can say that alternative reinforcers for behaviour other than sport are more powerful. The competition between reinforcers which occurs is likely to be between primary and secondary reinforcers. The primary reinforcers are those which satisfy bodily needs, it will be remembered, and these are likely to prove more effective in the control of behaviour. This is probably a major part of the reason for a lack of participation in sport for the majority of world population. Allied to this is the fact that even where some leisure exists there may not be the physical environmental requirements necessary for sport. Even though reinforcers may be available for sport, without the opportunity to participate, no reinforcement can be given.

If one is to believe the dire predictions for world population and resources, it is possible that sport may become increasingly a luxury behaviour which only a small minority, who are lucky enough to have available to them those primary reinforcers in sufficient abundance, will find the secondary reinforcers available from sport attractive. It is only a decade since the reverse predictions were *de rigeur* in sport and physical education. At that time, the optimistic predictions were that leisure and money were increasing and the time was forseeable when only a minority would have to work for a living. Physical educationists were just one group involved in leisure pursuits which were discussing the education of leisure society. Within western culture the optimistic predictions still appear to hold some validity. There is still an increase in leisure and there is an increase in money, prerequisites for sport participation. The pessimism is derived from predictions based on the third world, underdeveloped nations and the limits of resources. The new four horsemen of the apocalypse (as they have been called) progress, production, population and pollution, while becoming sufficiently threatening to cause alarm amongst the developed nations, have not yet reversed the trend towards greater leisure. Only when, and if, this trend is reversed is it likely that the field of sport will be affected in the developed world.

Since, for the majority, sport is a leisure activity we may feel that once a culture has provided for the basic necessities of life, there will be an automatic increase in participation in sport. This does not happen automatically. An increase in participation may occur simply because when time is available, the existing reinforcers for participation begin to exert some control. Skinner reflects:

> Leisure has long been associated with artistic, literary and scientific productivity. One must be at leisure to engage in these activities, and only a reasonably affluent society can support them on a broad scale. But leisure itself does not necessarily lead to art, literature, or science. Special cultural conditions are needed. Those who are concerned with the survival of their culture will therefore look closely at the contingencies which remain when exigent contingencies in daily life have been attenuated.

Skinner could have included sport in his list just as easily. It is the remaining contingencies which we are now trying to identify. Those 'exigent contingencies' remain within the developing nations.

Punishment in Sport

More important in our discussion of sport are the reasons for non-participation within the developed world. One of these reasons is the fact that sports behaviour is frequently punished. This has already been mentioned in brief in the last section. The punishment provided following a behaviour is likely to cause the suppression of that behaviour. If the punishment is intense the response may be eliminated from the organism's repertoire. As we have seen, punishment may take many different forms. There are some aversive consequences which are inherent within the activity itself. One cannot compete in a mile race without physical distress at the end. This physical stress may be sufficiently aversive to prevent further responding. What is perhaps more important is that the physical distress is greater in the endurance sports for the relative novice than the experienced participant. Part of the training process for endurance events is the tolerance of discomfort. The athlete who is well trained may suffer less, subjectively, from his exertions than the novice. Leaving aside

47

the unmeasurable and subjective aspects of the discomfort, it is certain that the well-trained athlete recovers more quickly from his exertion than the untrained. The essential point, therefore, is that the novice is punished for a longer period of time after a given piece of exercise. The more extensive punishment is also applied to a response (the skill or performance) which is less stable and which has a shorter history of reinforcement from other sources than is the case with the well-trained colleague. There is a high probability that under these circumstances a large proportion of people will soon give up endurance sports after first trying them. When alternative sports, offering the same reinforcements, are available a change from the endurance event is highly likely. It is also probable that a number of others will find the reinforcers available in other leisure activities of greater influence on their behaviour and terminate their participation in all sports because of their aversive experience with endurance events, a generalization effect.

One aspect of this process is the fact that, just as generalization occurs in the acquisition of responses, it also occurs in the termination of responses. We have already noted that a particular skill acquired in one context (under one set of stimulus conditions) is likely to occur when a similar but not identical situation arises. The stimuli which are associated with punishment develop a parallel function. Those stimuli which are not part of the punishment, but which are contiguously associated with it, are likely to come to act as signals to produce avoidance responses. In concrete terms, we can say that, if sporting activity has been punished for some reason, perhaps through the inherent punishers within the situation, not only may that behaviour be terminated or suppressed, but also when similar stimuli are presented, an avoidance response may occur. After receiving punishment for one sport, therefore, a large number of similar sports may be affected and participation in those sports may not occur simply because of the avoidance reaction to the stimuli with which they are associated. I feel fairly certain that this phenomenon accounts for many of the non-participants amongst adults. Performance in sports at school has been punished in some way and the avoidance has generalized to a large range of sports. The degree of generalization will depend on a number of factors, not least of which is the intensity of the punishment provided. One finds that adults who do not participate in sports are more likely to begin indulging in those sports with which they have no previous experience than those which they have directly tried. For example, many inveterate non-sportsmen may take up golf later in life. There are reinforcers which are available for participation in this sport. Probably of greater significance is that this sport takes place in a totally different context from those sports which have, perhaps, been previously punished.

To return to the idea of inherent punishers. All body-contact sports have the potential to inflict punishment upon the participant. The obvious case is boxing in which the whole sport revolves around presenting as many painful stimuli to one's opponent as possible. The same is true, however, in many team game situations. Compensating reinforcement may not be sufficient for many people to maintain the behaviour in the face of the punishment presented. For this reason the behaviour may cease to occur. Sports injuries are so common and their effect on participation so well known, that we need not dwell on the issue.

There are other punishing events which may be inherent to the sport which are concerned with physical aspects of the environment. We have seen that, to some people, controlled fear and the stimulation provided by fear-producing situations may be reinforcing. There are others to whom this fear is completely aversive. No matter how well-controlled the situation is, there are some people who would never attempt a rock-climb. The same may apply to underwater swimming or scuba diving and all those situations which contain an element of danger. Participation is associated with the emotional response of fear which is an aversive state for a proportion of people. Having the opportunity to perform it they never accept.

This should not lead us to conclude that the modification of this behaviour is impossible. If we take one example, we can make the point clear. The fear of heights associated with rock-climbing can be manipulated by means of operant conditioning. Many so-called phobias have been treated by the application of shaping and successive approximations on the basis of positive reinforcement. An example of an experiment will clarify this point. Johnston et al (1966) applied operant conditioning techniques to the behaviour of an inactive child who particularly avoided a climbing frame. Over a period of nine days secondary reinforcers of attention and smiling and praise were used to manipulate the behaviour of the child. Systematic shaping of the behaviour brought the child closer and closer to the climbing frame and eventually led to high levels of activity on this equipment. After the conditioning period the child spent over sixty-five per cent of his outside activity time on the climbing frame whereas before conditioning, the baseline frequency of this operant was less than one per cent.

Our description is therefore an account of what currently exists in terms of behaviour patterns and is not meant to imply an unalterable state of affairs.

A number of outdoor sports are also subject to the rigours of climate. Anyone who has been forced onto a soccer field in a snowstorm in shorts and shirt will testify to the punishing qualities of the situation. Falling into an icy river while canoeing or being caught in a thunderstorm while hill-walking are other examples of consequences which may result in the termination of responding for numbers of participants. This could be the case if the punishment regularly accompanies the response, but if the punishment is intense enough it may have an immediate influence upon participation; and again is likely to be off-set by the reinforcers in the situation.

Just as the social context may produce reinforcement so may it provide punishment. We used the illustration of the nagging wife as a negative reinforcer in the last section. Family comments of this kind may be an effective punisher as well. If the behaviour of one marriage partner does not receive the approval of the other then that withholding of approval may constitute extinction. If disapproval is vociferous, and regularly follows upon performance, it is legitimate to consider it as a punisher. This kind of punishment may lead to the termination of that behaviour in due course, or at least its suppression. The application of verbal punishment is frequently found amongst peers and this may be as important as familial influences. In part this reflects a mind-body dualism which retains some significant role in our culture. The aesthete, the academic and the ascetic are often prone to denigrate participation in sport. Presumably this is a reflection of their own histories of reinforcement in sport. If we consider them in their role of controller rather than controlled, however, their verbal behaviour toward another may have a significant impact upon participation. They may punish the colleague who participates in sports with jibes and sneers which are both unpleasant and may also signify to the participant that his acceptance within the group is in jeopardy. This may be off-set, of course, by the reinforcers we have already considered, but nevertheless may be a significant factor. The author is aware of academics, for example, who have kept their participation in sport a secre rather than suffer these jibes.

Punishment in verbal form is seldom unselective. Many sports may receive the sanction of peers when other sports do not. Those sports which contain the prestigious label we discussed in the last chapter may not receive punishment, whereas the less prestigious may be treated unmercifully. Nor is the punishment restricted to general condemnation. The verbal punishers may be provided only for inferior performance. The athlete who never wins may find the verbal punishment for his behaviour occurring not only from his non-participating friends, but even from those with whom he participates in the sport. Perhaps this is particularly true with the younger age groups who indulge in sport. A child who always fails in his sport (by failing we mean failing to win) may be showing improvement in his level of performance and deriving many reinforcers from his participation and yet receive verbal punishment through mockery, teasing and contempt from his peers. If this continues, the behaviour is likely to be suppressed and reinforcement derived elsewhere.

There is a strong influence within our culture which, however much it is decried, remains firmly entrenched. The work ethic or Protestant ethic is a cultural phenomenon which has permeated the structure of much of our culture. Within this ethic there is the component which regards play and leisure activities as inappropriate behaviours. An individual who devotes a considerable amount of time to his sport may well find that he is censured simply on this basis. Cultures and behavioural aspects of cultures have been dichotomized as continuous or discontinuous in terms of their behavioural demands. A continuous culture is one in which the same behavioural demands are made throughout life, whereas a discontinuous culture is one in which the behaviour demanded changes with age. For example most western cultures are relatively continuous with respect to sexual modesty, but are discontinuous with respect to sexual activity. In terms of sport, it is worth pointing out that our culture is relatively discontinuous. Play is often seen as a childhood phenomenon which is to be put away when the individual reaches maturity. That is, playing behaviours such as sport, which are fruitless in material terms, are punished as childish behaviours. How often does one hear from non-sympathetic observers the statement that they cannot understand how grown men could spend an afternoon chasing a lump of leather? The implication is that it is perfectly understandable that children should behave in this way, but not understandable that adults should. The imprecation that sport is childish is an effective verbal punisher which society can use for people who participate. The discontinuity is revealing, since it does not occur in all cultures. The relationship of this discontinuity to the Protestant work ethic is probably very close. It is obvious that for a number of reasons societies often provide verbal punishments for sports participation on the grounds that it reflects some immaturity on the part of the participant.

There are also sex differences in the degree to which punishment is applied to sporting behaviour. Sport is not only considered childish by some sections of society, but is also considered unladylike. There are differences in the degree to which verbal punishment may be applied in different sports, but generally speaking the sportswoman is likely to find more verbal punishers from the social context than the male. This is allied to a difference in the reinforcements available between the sexes. Females tend to receive lower levels of reinforcement for participation and greater levels of censure when they are actively involved. At the highest levels of sports performance, the woman tends to be paid less than the equivalent male. This reflects the fact that this society values the performance of males more highly. The general public is prepared to pay for watching males in greater amounts than females. At other levels, the reinforcements provided through social approval are much smaller. The girls passing through school and beyond do not receive the universal approval awarded to their male contemporaries.

When these two factors are taken together (greater public censure and lower levels of reinforcement) it is not surprising that females should participate to a much smaller extent in sport. Perhaps for females there is greater discontinuity in the behavioural demands within this society. Puberty represents a more significant change in behavioural expectations for girls than boys. The minority which regards sport as proper childhood behaviour for boys is probably smaller than the group which regards it as the only proper time for sports activities for girls.

Although punishment is a factor in terminating behaviour, it was pointed out in the first chapter that it is only effective in very limited circumstances in totally eradicating that behaviour. When the punishers are removed the behaviour is apt to reappear again. We certainly find that the behaviour of many is resistant to the punishment which society provides for sporting behaviour and to the inherent punishers within sports themselves. Yet punishment is probably more effective in real-life situations than it is in the laboratory situation. For one thing, the human has a control over his environment which the laboratory rat cannot exert. The rat is placed back in the experimental situation repeatedly—a situation in which there are strong associations with the production of a particular response. Even though that response was previously punished in that situation, nevertheless it was learned there and those associations may serve to maintain a tendency to respond. In the case of man, punishment within a particular situation may produce an avoidance of the situation. The sportsman may not go near the scene of the punishment again. In the same way, when punishment is being used with laboratory animals there are seldom alternative responses which are reinforced. With man, there are many such alternatives which may receive reinforcement. The punishment may be more effective when there are alternative responses which receive positive reinforcement. It is found in the laboratory, when this kind of experiment is performed, that the punished behaviour is terminated more quickly than when no alternative responses are available.

The Extinction Process in Sport

It is probable that, although punishment in its various forms may account for a decline in sports participation to some extent, other phenomena may also be important. Extinction is the process in which responding tends to cease after reinforcement is terminated. We have seen that the most obvious case is when the professional ceases to be paid for his participation. Amateurs also tend to reduce and stop their participation with age. In individual sports this can be analyzed in a very straightforward manner. Much of the reinforcement in sport is derived through winning and being successful. The probability of receiving this kind of reinforcement is likely to decline with age. Many of the reinforcers from sport are associated with success. When these begin to decline, there begins the process of extinction. The frequency of responding slows and eventually the behaviour does not occur again. The process may take an extremely long time if the response has been learned on the basis of high levels of reinforcement and especially if some schedule of reinforcement, such as variable ratio schedule, has been used to maintain the performance. Nevertheless, the behaviour is likely to terminate eventually if competitive success and its associated social approval has been the major form of reinforcement. From the reduction of participation with age this appears to be a reasonable account.

There are those who continue to participate in their particular sport long after they have ceased to be successful in any competitive sense. These performers must represent those whose reinforcement comes from different sources. The stimulation, the healthful feelings, the social context may all remain in some sports, even when success is lacking and may serve to maintain the behaviour well into old age. There is also likely to be a parallel between the removal of the reinforcement of success and the application of punishment. As the participant in many body-contact sports gets older, he tends to receive more of the inherent punishers within the sport, to suffer more at the hands of his opponents, and his giving up the sport may be due to both of these factors operating together.

The extinction analysis becomes more difficult in the team-game situation. Here the performer does not feel his own lack of success in such a direct manner. A team may continue to be successful in spite of a less capable member. Where each team member has a measurable performance, the success of anyone may be obvious and continued failure may result in extinction. For example, in cricket or baseball the individual's lack of success may be easily accountable. It is less easy where a total team effort is involved. In soccer it is difficult to assess the contribution of an individual in a measurable way. Especially if the team is successful, it would be an extraordinary observer who could rank the team's individual performances. Nevertheless, it is likely that the lack of success of an individual will eventually become obvious and extinction will be accompanied by punishment. The rest of the team may make it obvious to the individual that his quality of behaviour is no longer acceptable by both words and signs. In the professional and upper level amateur team games his performance is also likely to be punished by dismissal from the team.

As in the case of punishment and learning it is important to remember that extinction also generalizes. We noted in the first section that if a response has been learned under one set of stimulus conditions it is likely that similar stimuli will also serve to elicit the response. In other words, one can suggest that in learning to respond under condition A an organism has *thereby* also learned to make that response under condition B. The reverse also applies. If an extinction process is achieved under A, extinction is thereby accomplished if B is presented. The removal of reinforcement from the sportsman is likely to have a wider impact on his behaviour than simply on the specific sport itself.

In some respects the effects on behaviour of punishment and extinction are very similar. They may both lead to a termination of responding. It has been suggested that the processes are in many ways identical. For an organism to have reinforcement withheld, after it has previously been received for a specific response, may be regarded as a form of punishment. But the behaviours associated with the processes may be quite different. The application of an aversive stimulus following a response is likely to be associated with emotional side effects, whereas non-reinforcement may not. In other words, punishment may be paired with escape behaviours whereas extinction is not. In some highly restricted situations the beginning of an extinction process may actually produce an increase in the strength of the response. This has been called a frustration effect and it may be produced in the following way. A rat is placed in a double runway designed so that the animal can run one half after which it receives reinforcement. Then the next half of the runway is opened so that the animal can continue to a second goal. When the running response has been well learned and an asymptote has been reached, we can begin the extinction trials by removing the reinforcement. The result is that the animal tends to run faster in the second runway than before.

In lay terms we can say that the frustration produced by being unreinforced in the first goal box has an ergogenic effect on performance in the second runway. If the rat continues to find no reinforcement the extinction of the response will gradually occur.

We may draw some parallels with human behaviour. If success is the reinforcement for sports behaviour, we may find that increased levels of responding occur when failure first results. The extinction process does not necessarily begin immediately, but the effect of initial failures may be renewed efforts of greater strength than those previously produced. Only if failure in the sport continues is extinction likely to occur.

Omission Training

There are additional laboratory techniques which are relevant to the non-participation of adults in sport. We mentioned these in chapter one and have hinted at them subsequently. Omission training is the label given to a process by which an animal is given positive reinforcement for not performing. In the laboratory we can train an animal through shaping and positive reinforcement to perform a particular response. Once the behaviour is established we may cease to reward it (begin extinction) but also give positive reinforcement every time the animal does not respond. The animal is rewarded for failing to produce a previously learned response. During our discussion of sport we have frequently referred to the concept of competing reinforcers. These are reinforcements for responses other than sport, which may lead to a reduction in sports behaviour. In this case, however, we are linking extinction to positive reinforcement which is contingent upon not responding. There is no doubt that this kind of reinforcement may be presented to many performers, especially from those with whom they are in social contact but who are non-participants. One can imagine, for example, a non-participating wife giving generous social reinforcement to her sports-loving husband, when he stays at home on Saturday afternoon. This is not reinforcement for doing something else, but is reinforcement for not participating in sport. In order to receive the reinforcement, he must simply be passive. When the husband is reinforced in his sport, we have competition between reinforcers, but when extinction begins and he is no longer receiving his reinforcement for sport, the extinction of the sports behaviour may be drastically facilitated by this omission training.

The nature of the process by which sports behaviour is terminated is, therefore, very complex. Each individual is likely to derive idiosyncratic reinforcements from his sport and the termination of whatever are the important reinforcers for him will eventually lead to the reduction in participation. If we wish to make generalizations concerning the nature of the reinforcements it is possible to analyze the extinction process. The application of the generalization to an individual may not always work, however, since we may not have identified the reinforcements accurately. The generalizations are also likely to vary depending on the sport. There exist many sports in which there is little overt competition, for example. Our analysis that failure to win is an important element in the termination of behaviour would not be justifiable in this case and we must look for other causal relationships for our explanation.

Retirement

There is one category of reduction in sports behaviour that is not explained by the analyses that we have made so far. This is the case of the undefeated champion who retires or the Olympic athlete who, after his greatest success, decides to compete no more. These sportsmen are still at the peak of their reinforcement. Their responding has received bigger and bigger reinforcements and their responding is firmly established. To quit at this point seems to defy all the generalizations we have made concerning a gradual reduction in performance after reinforcements are terminated. The reinforcements are still being presented and yet the behaviour is no longer produced.

This presents a difficult problem for the behaviourist to explain, but some account is possible. Firstly, the champion may not quit completely. He may retire from top class competition, but the behaviour of participation be maintained at some lower level for a considerable period of time. The champion swimmer or athlete, who no longer takes any active part in his sport after retirement from top-class competition, must be quite a rarity. In one sense, we may be misled by the term retirement into thinking that it means total non-participation. This may not be the case at all. The second assumption which is made is that the champion who retires is at the peak of his reinforcement. This is probably true in most material terms, but the Olympic athlete is also at the peak of punishment. The arduous training which accompanies top class performance may become increasingly aversive. As the Olympic Games have gained in prestige value, the quality of performance has increased and the demands in terms of effort from those who participate in the Games has increased proportionally. This work may become very aversive for the competitor. Having received the reinforcement of Olympic victory, the prospect of future participation may be influenced more by the aversive stimuli associated with the training process than by future reinforcements from his success. One aspect of this behaviour is that in such events as the Olympic Games the duration of non-reinforcement following each reinforcement is quite considerable. One could, for example, liken the Olympic Games to a fixed interval reinforcement schedule. As we saw in the first section, one of the consequences of fixed interval reinforcement is the post reinforcement pause. A general break in performance is to be anticipated in any event. No doubt all athletes take a break after a performance of this kind. If there are aversive associations with the sport (the mammoth training schedules) these may be sufficient to terminate the behaviour altogether.

It is interesting to note how many of such champions, who have received part of their reinforcement on a fixed interval basis, make a comeback after so-called retirement. This phenomenon is directly analogous to the behaviour of organisms on fixed interval schedules. Following reinforcement the organism 'retires' for the post-reinforcement pause, only to begin responding later in the interval.

There is one additional point which needs to be made. The reinforcement for Olympic champions comes in part from social approval. The reinforcement of social approval for the champion is no longer contingent upon responding. The television exposure and accolades awarded to Mark Spitz, for example, could be thought of as reinforcement for simply appearing. No doubt if Mark Spitz never swims again he will continue to receive this esteem. In this sense the reinforcement is still provided without participation. To summarize, therefore, the champion who retires at the peak of behaviour is likely to continue some performance and also likely to continue to receive a large proportion of the reinforcement. The highest level of competition may have been terminated by the aversive consequences of arduous training.

Individual Differences and Behavioural Analysis

There is a further aspect of failure to participate in sport or the termination of this behaviour which remains to be discussed. This is the question of physical limitations of the organism. Individual differences is a subject which has been little examined by operant conditioners. The reasons for this are probably twofold. The determinism which is an inherent part of behaviourism has led to a concentration on those aspects of the environment which control behaviour. The underlying assumption is not that all animals of a species are identical at birth, but that general principles of the influence of the environment from birth onwards may be discovered. Because the control of organisms by the effect of environment is the area in which the behaviourist concentrates, he has been accused of promulgating an entirely empiricist view. This is not true and it is perfectly possible to reconcile the goals of the differential psychologist with those of the experimental behaviourist, as we shall see. The second major reason for the concentration of the behaviourist on environmental influences in general, rather than on individual differences, is the nature of the subjects used for his experiments. In order to determine the extent of environmental influence, it is essential that a close control is maintained over the environment of the subjects. This is only possible with infrahuman organisms. These animals, usually rats or pigeons, are bred for laboratory purposes and are therefore often very similar genetically. Indeed, in order to assess the contribution of environmental influence it is often essential that the animals be very similar genetically. The bulk of research in basic operant conditioning is, therefore, performed on animals in which individual differences with respect to the tasks to be learned are relatively minor.

The misrepresentation of Skinner on this issue has come about through a very simple series of steps which have been made both by his critics and to a lesser extent by his supporters. The noted differential psychologist Jensen (1973) discussed this problem in detail and he points out that it is well established that

> . . . Practically any bit of behaviour responds to reinforcement contingencies. This is impressive raw fact: reinforcement contingencies change behaviour. The next step, taken by so many Skinnerians, is not fact: that is, when we observe a behavioural difference between two organisms, we may say the difference must be due to different histories of reinforcement. And one can always point to circumstantial differences in individual histories, which adds to the plausibility. But this second step, we know, is both logically and factually wrong.

Jensen continues to explain that individual differences are important in any complete description of man and argues that the only significant point of distinction between differential psychologists and the experimental behaviourist is the area of concentration:

> So behaviourism really has no justification for excluding differential psychology, other than the legitimate grounds of a division of scientific labor, or for presupposing that all the subject matter of differential psychology can simply be subsumed under the study of reinforcement contingencies (Jensen, 1973).

Jensen's concern is mainly with the influence of different levels of intelligence on performance. He makes the point, in very telling fashion, that no matter how efficiently the reinforcement contingencies in education are handled there is no possibility that equality of performance can be achieved. The same point can be made with equal validity with regard to performance in sport. Inherited physical traits are likely to restrict participation in some sports to groups of individuals who are genetically endowed with some specific physical characteristcs. The use of any system of reinforcement, no matter how efficient, will never make those who do not possess this characteristic into successful participants in these events. For example various gross inherited malfunctions may make participation in any active sport an impossibility. The child born with an untreatable heart condition may not perform in any sports no matter what reinforcements are used.

Generally speaking, the inherited characteristics of an individual serve to interact with the reinforcement contingencies to produce a choice of sport rather than a choice between non-participation and participation. After participating in a sport and finding reinforcement, a child may continue with the behaviour, only to find that because of genetically determined characteristics the reinforcements gradually cease. The ensuing extinction process is an indirect function of genetic factors. A personal anecdote may be used to illustrate the point. In his youth, the author held the All-England under fifteen eighty yards hurdles record. In retrospect the reinforcements for his hurdling were very significant in shaping his behaviour. With the esteem derived from school, peers and family one could predict continuation of this behaviour. However, at age fourteen the author had reached his adult height (5ft 8in). As the hurdles got higher and the distances between them longer, and the author's legs remained the same size, there was a gradual reduction in the reinforcements provided for hurdling. By age eighteen this bit of behaviour had been totally extinguished. The loss of reinforcement was due to the genetic limitation on growth.

This factor is of great significance in determining the sports in which an individual may find his reinforcement. Many sports have physical requirements which one section of the population does not possess. This is most obvious in those sports which Knapp (1963) has labelled as being at the habit end of the continuum of sports. Those sports which are based on the repetition of a mechanically perfect set of movements, such as discus throwing, are at this end of the continuum whereas those which are heavily concerned with superiority of strategy are labelled as lying at the perceptual end of the continuum. The physical demands of a particular sport, at the habit end of the continuum, make only a narrow band of somatotypes optimal. Those not so endowed will find their reinforcements gradually disappearing. This is true in many track and field events. High jumpers, shot-putters, discus throwers as well as weight-lifters and gymnasts are all sportsmen who must have certain physical characteristics in order to succeed. The demands in terms of physique are not nearly so stringent in those sports at the perceptual end of the continuum. The varieties of somatotype one finds in soccer players, tennis players and in many team sports indicate the breadth of somatotypes which may receive reinforcement in these sports. Knapp rightly stresses the fact that this is a continuum and sports vary in the degree to which strategy plays a role and the degree to which habit plays a role. There are also likely to be different degrees to which a sport is dependent upon somatotype. For example, basketball as a team sport, must be labelled as lying at the perceptual end of the continuum and yet the probability of being reinforced in that sport is highly correlated with genetically determined physical characteristics. Similarly, different sports may have variations in physical demands depending upon the position within the game. Thus, American football and rugby football have different demands in terms of physique for playing one position rather than another. Reinforcements are likely to be awarded on the basis of performance and performance may be a function of genetically determined factors in varying degrees.

This factor may be important in terms of determining the choice of sport an individual makes, but it has wide implications. As a generalization, greater success in sport is more probable for those with a mesomorphic somatotype than for others, or at least those with a high mesomorphic component in the somatotype. They are likely to be successful and to receive reinforcements for a larger proportion of sports than are other somatotypes. Since not all children are exposed to all sports, the probability of participation being limited to those who have a mesomorphic somatotype is quite high. There are obvious exceptions to this, but, of different somatotypes, one should predict higher levels of participation amongst mesomorphs than the rest and this does appear to be the case. The effect of this reinforcement provided for a particular somatotype also generalizes. The mesomorph is likely to participate in other sports upon reaching adulthood, because he has been reinforced in his school sports. Conversely, the ectomorph or endomorph is less likely to participate in sports, because of the lack of reinforcement he has received in similar situations.

There is an additional factor related to genetically determined physique. This is the rate of physical growth. There are variations amongst adolescents in the age at which mature size is reached. The so-called 'early developer' has an enormous advantage over his peers in sport, because of his size and weight. Since early developers receive reinforcement due to their size, they will have firmly developed tendencies to respond at later stages. The early developer is likely to experience fewer of the punishing aspects of sport and greater levels of reinforcement for his sports activity. He is more likely to continue in the behaviour for a longer period of time. The late developer may have experienced a sport, at say thirteen, and been soundly beaten at it, not because of differences in skill so much as the fact that his peers are bigger and heavier than he is. This experience of punishment and low reinforcement levels may be influential in determining later participation when the imbalance in height and weight has been changed. As with the case of the non-mesomorph, this influence may be affective upon other sports, as well as the one in which the punishment and failure were derived. The stimulus environments associated with sport are often very similar and an avoidance response may be made to a new sport because of the similarity of stimuli with those presented during the aversive experience. The late developer is, therefore, much less likely to become an active participant in all sports than is the early developer.

Obviously these statements are probabilistic rather than empirical facts. Individual reinforcement histories will have considerable impact on these considerations. It would be interesting to determine whether this prediction is borne out by a survey of sport participation and its relationship to age of puberty.

The above analysis seems reasonable for males, but the probabilities associated with physical development for females may be quite different. Since females receive lower levels of reinforcement for sport at all ages and a higher level of verbal punishment for participation, the question of age of puberty is probably a less relevant factor. Other aspects of the reinforcement contingencies, such as parental approval, may be of greater relative importance to participation. An additional factor is that greater size and weight may not be such an advantage with females as with males. The female at puberty shows a growth spurt in terms of height and weight, as do males, but a larger proportion of the increase in weight is due to the accumulation of fat tissue, which may be disadvantageous in sports' situations. Additionally, a smaller proportion of female sports depend on height and weight or give advantages for this reason. For example, there is a notable absence of body contact sports for females, which give great advantage to those who are heavier and taller. The late-developing female may, therefore, experience fewer of the deterrents to participation than the late developing male and the relationship between developmental rate and future participation may be much lower.

Abilities and Reinforcement

In our discussion of individual differences so far we have limited ourselves to those which are almost directly the product of genetic factors. Height and weight, developmental rate and somatotype are susceptible to change due to experience, but the modifications which can be made tend to be relatively minor. There are, however, a number of traits in which there is an interaction between inheritance and environment. This interaction may not be analyzable into components. For example, there are many traits which are valuable in specific sports, but whether an individual is equipped with greater or lesser amounts of these traits because of genetic endowment or because of his experience and the reinforcement contingencies of his history, may not be determinable. To put this in concrete terms, we could use the example of reaction time. There are individual differences in reaction time. This is a fact. There are also many sports in which superior reaction time is correlated with performance. One may think, for example, of squash rackets, goal keeping at ice hockey, table tennis and many others. We can speculate, therefore, that those with superior reaction time are more likely to receive reinforcement for participation in these sports than those with a slower reaction time. Whether reaction time is attributable to genetic factors is not known. An individual who lacks a number of these traits, which form sub-components of sports skills may therefore fail to receive the reinforcement of winning in any of them. In this case, failure to participate is likely to be a product of non-reinforcement, but the non-reinforcement may be attributed to factors inherent to the performer, whether acquired at some earlier date or inherited.

What are these sub-components which may have such an effect on possible participation? A vast amount of research literature has been accumulated by E. A. Fleishman and his associates and followers. Their work has consisted of analyzing performance of individuals on various artificial tasks, using factor analytic techniques. With this method, it is possible to identify sub-components of performance which are relevant to specific tasks. The relative contributions of these components may then be assessed in other skills. In this way, Fleishman and his co-workers maintain it is possible to pretest subjects on small artificial tasks and predict from the results the rate of acquisition and final level of success achievable on some major skill. The factors found to be relevant were divided by Fleishman into two sets, those relevant to fine motor skills and those relevant to gross motor skills. These factors may be listed and the reader is referred to Fleishman (1966) for a summary article. In fine motor skills much of the variance between individuals was found to be a product of differences in control precision, multilimb coordination, response orientation, reaction time, speed of arm movement, rate control. manual dexterity, finger dexterity, arm-hand steadiness, wrist, finger speed and aiming. Fleishman called these factors 'abilities' and suggested that they are general components of skills. In any new skill-learning situation, an individual will bring these abilities with him and they will serve to determine his level of performance in part. There is also a specific component in skill, which may be regarded as the unpredictable element. The magnitude of the contribution of this specific component varies from skill to skill. For gross motor activities, Fleishman identified the following abilities; extent flexibility, dynamic flexibility, static strength, trunk strength, gross body coordination, gross body equilibrium and stamina. These are components which will, to a greater or lesser extent, contribute to the performance of a specific skill. Having measured an individual's level of ability on these factors, we have grounds for predicting his performance in a specific skill, provided we can assess the sub-components of that skill. Again, there is a specific component in gross motor skills which cannot be predicted for an individual before he actually begins his performance of the skill.

To return to our theme, we can note that the factors outlined above are independent of each other. That is, a subject may have a high score on one of these factors and a low score on another. Knowing the level of one factor does not enable us to predict the level on another. When an individual is given exposure to a sport, his level in those abilities relevant to that sport may, in large measure, predict his success and hence the reinforcement he will derive. Since the factors are independent of one another, it may be a long process of search before an individual attempts that sport for which he has the appropriate or optimal abilities. This implies repeated exposure and repeated failure to find reinforcement. The general tendency to indulge in sport may have been extinguished long before the appropriate sport is tried. In the same way, an individual may have low levels on all of the factors outlined above. The result of this is that success may never be achieved in any sport and the behaviour become extinguished. This is the case of what used to be called the motor moron, who is apparently incapable of learning sports skills.

The question of individual differences and underlying abilities adds a new dimension of determinism. As we pointed out earlier, the degree to which level of ability is genetically determined is difficult to assess. Obviously in those factors outlined by Fleishman, stamina, strength and flexibility are modified by experience. But, what is not known is the extent coordination, reaction time and equilibrium may be modified in this way. If an ability is modifiable, it is probable that its influence on participation will not be so great. The appropriate ability may be developed through participation in the sport. If we over-simplify for the sake of clarity, we could use the following example. Suppose that sport A has a specific component and for successful participation it also demands high levels of stamina and strength. The prognosis for someone who was weak and lacked stamina would be low, but through participation in that sport his level on those abilities may be altered and success be achieved. The problem, of course, would be that since initial experiences in the sport would involve failure the behaviour may be extinguished before the abilities had been developed. Fleishman points out that those abilities which underlie fine motor performance are relatively stable in adulthood and one could estimate that the same would be true for those underlying gross motor skills, if any survey of the general population were accomplished. The fact that testing revealed them to be relatively stable does not imply that they are unmodifiable. It may be the case that since failure accompanies attempts at those skills for which the individual does not already have the appropriate abilities, he seldom persists in those skills which would lead to their acquisition. The fact that abilities appear to be relatively stable may be no more than a reflection of the contingencies of reinforcement surrounding the application of those abilities.

This speculation appears to have been tested to only a very minor extent. Any indication of the stability of a trait tends to be used as evidence that it is an

61

aspect of autonomous man or inherited, whereas we have indicated that it may be just as subject to the contingencies of reinforcement and punishment as those more obviously modifiable aspects of behaviour.

The novice in a task is faced with a novel situation in which he must bring to bear previous experience. It is also found, through factor analytic studies, that those abilities which produce initial superiority may not be those which are of paramount importance at later stages. In other words, the factor structure within a particular skill may change as the level of skill rises. Fleishman and co-workers have shown this in a number of studies. The abilities which account for level of performance vary in the proportion of their contribution with the level of skill achieved. For example, Fleishman and Rich (1963), in what has become a very famous study, showed that proprioceptive sensitivity is more important at later stages in skill than at earlier stages. The significance of this kind of finding to participation in sport may be very great indeed. What it means is that those with the necessary abilities for early superiority will find immediate reinforcement for their attempts at a particular skill. If they also have the necessary abilities for superior performance, or can acquire them, they may find sufficient reinforcement for them to go on and eventually reach the upper levels of competition. Of greater relevance to this discussion, however, is the plight of the novice who has a high capacity in those abilities which are necessary for eventual supremacy in performance, but has only low levels of those abilities necessary for initial superiority. Let us again oversimplify in order to illustrate. Suppose that quality of manual dexterity is the single most important factor in the early stages of acquiring a particular skill. Those with high levels of manual dexterity will find that they receive reinforcement for participation in this skill. Once the skill is learned, let us say that the set of movements has been acquired, the determinant of ultimate level of performance may be reaction time. These two factors are independent of each other. For the individual who has both good manual dexterity and a fast reaction time, there is obviously no problem. He will receive reinforcement for his performance and continue to do so. For the person with poor reaction time and dexterity the analysis of behaviour may also be predicted easily. He will not receive reinforcement and we should find eventually that his responding extinguishes. The problem comes with the novice who has good reaction time and poor manual dexterity. We should predict that this individual would spend a long time in the initial stages of skill learning, gradually acquiring the movements necessary for the skill. Having once learned these movements, his superior reaction time may lead him to a high level of success. This analysis forgets the importance of the consequences of the initial responses. The fact that he receives no reinforcement, or fails, in his early attempts may lead to the extinction of the behaviour before he reaches the stage at which his superior reaction time becomes valuable. Conversely, the subject with good manual dexterity and poor reaction time may find that his reinforcements decrease as his level of skill increases. He will find that amongst other novices he shines as the best performer and receives the reinforcement appropriate to this position. However, as others slowly acquire the initial skills, he finds his own relative standing slipping and others with superior reaction time overtaking his performance. This performer is then likely to terminate his behaviour as the extinction process has its effect.

This example is an oversimplification, but the same principles are likely to apply in the more complex sport skill situations of real-life. Those performers who have the necessary underlying capacities for ultimate superior performance may terminate their behaviour before this becomes apparent and those with the necessary capacities for initial superiority may find their participation reinforced in a decreasing fashion until the extinction of the response finally occurs.

When discussing participation and the reinforcements which produced this, it was necessary to point out that modelling or imitative behaviour was not directly explainable through traditional reinforcement principles and to add the possibility of participation due to this process to our list of reinforcement contingencies. By the same token, it is necessary to add imitative behaviour to the reasons for non-participation in sport. The child who produces imitation of models who participate in sport may have his counterpart in children who do not participate in sport. They may be using non-participating parents as models, for example. The same argument also applies to these children. They are likely to have developed generalized tendencies to imitate their parents since the parents have reinforced imitation of adult behaviours.

Personality

It has been a frequent observation made by sportsmen and non-sportsmen alike that personality characteristics are influential in the selection of sports. Distinct personality types appear to select particular sports with great frequency. Superficially, there also appears to be a personality-type who participates in sports in general.

We may conclude that people of a particular personality-type are likely to find reinforcement in sport in general or in some specific sports, whereas others are not. Before we can consider this question we must consider what the term personality means. In our analysis of man and his participation in sport we have concentrated upon his behaviour. When we observe that certain categories of behaviour appear with some regularity in the repertoire of an individual, we may describe this individual with a single label which covers all of those behaviours. If a boy fights at school regularly, pulls girls' hair and does material damage, we may describe him as 'aggressive,' or as being an 'aggressive personality.' What is not permissible in a behavioural analysis, is to say that he fights *because* of an aggressive personality. Again the problem is one of reification. There is a tendency to describe a set of behaviours with a label and then use the label in order to explain the behaviour. Often the process is taken one stage further and personality is described as an attribute of autonomous man. Any complete behavioural analysis must eventually describe the behaviours in terms of the contingencies which generated them, or identify any genetic components in behaviour and their interaction with those contingencies. Skinner (1971) suggests that this goal is already partly accomplished:

Behaviour which operates upon the environment to produce consequences ('operant' behaviour) can be studied by arranging environments in which specific consequences are contingent upon it. The contingencies under investigation have become steadily more complex, and one by one they are taking over the explanatory functions previously assigned to personalities, state of mind, feelings, traits of character, purposes, and intentions.

The goal of behavioural description is not achieved yet and in order to consider the observation that personality correlates with sport we must use the evidence that is available. However, we must neither fall into the trap of reification nor make reference to autonomous man in this description.

One of the additional pitfalls in the analysis of the relationship between personality and participation is the temptation to regard correlations as causal relationships. When a correlation is established we cannot determine, without additional evidence, in which direction causality may exist. In the literature of sport one can find assumptions that the correlation is causal in both directions. For example, it used to be common to see statements concerning the virtue of sports as character builders. The assumption was made that participation in a sport influenced personality—produced honesty, cooperativeness, determination, fair play and a lot of other desirable traits. More recently there has been a tendency to suggest the reverse, that we choose to indulge in sports because we are active and sociable and determined etc. So far as the author is aware neither viewpoint has ever been substantiated empirically and we are left with a conundrum of correlation which may only be solved by massive longitudinal studies.

There is one line of argument concerning personality which does fit into the behavioural analysis that we have made so far. Hans Eysenck has conducted, with his associates, numerous tests of personality using the same kinds of factor analytical methods that were discussed in connection with Fleishman's work. Using an analysis of this kind, Eysenck has divided personality into three components which he claims are relatively independent of each other. These components are extraversion-introversion, stability-neuroticism and a psychotism scale. If we describe an individual in terms of his position on these scales we have, according to Eysenck, accounted for a large proportion of the difference between individuals. In other words, we can describe individuals adequately by reference to just three scores. It is his contention that analyzing the scores into smaller and smaller sub-sections will explain only insignificant amounts of additional variance between people.

The scale which is most relevant in this context is the extraversion-introversion scale. After the administration of the personality test an individual is placed somewhere along this scale. Although the extremes of the scale tend to be discussed to a greater extent, the majority of people do not fall at extremes and cluster in the center in much the same way as when we measure other psychological attributes such as intelligence. In order to describe the personality differences represented by this scale, it is, however,customary to talk about the extreme cases. We can use Eysenck's (1965) own description:

The typical extravert is sociable, likes parties, has many friends, needs to have people to talk to, and does not like reading or studying by himself. He craves excitement, takes chances, often sticks his neck out, acts on the spur of the moment, and is generally an impulsive individual. He is fond of practical jokes, always has a ready answer, and optimistic, and likes to 'laugh and be merry.' He prefers to keep moving and doing things, tends to be aggressive, and loses his temper quickly. . . The typical introvert, on the other hand, is a quiet, retiring sort of person, introspective, fond of books rather than people; he is reserved and distant except with intimate friends. He tends to plan ahead, looks before he leaps, and distrusts the impulse of the moment. He does not like excitement, takes matters of everyday life with proper seriousness, and likes a well-ordered mode of life. He keeps his feelings under close control, seldom behaves in an aggressive manner, and does not lose his temper easily. He is reliable, somewhat pessimistic, and places great value on ethical standards.

This description coincides very closely with the lay usage of the terms. What is important from our point of view is the fact that the extravert appears to demand stimulation to a greater degree than the introvert. In other words, the extravert appears to produce those kinds of responses which result in greater levels of stimulation. We have already discussed the fact that stimulation can be thought of as a reinforcement, particularly when an organism has been deprived. It is now apparent that there exist individual differences in the degree to which individuals demand stimulation.

Since sport provides stimulation it is to be anticipated that this will provide greater reinforcement for extraverts. They have a greater potency for the extravert as a reinforcer. It is not surprising that the lay opinion of sportsmen is that they are generally an extraverted bunch and this is also the finding from personality surveys.

At this point we are invoking a motivational explanation. It is suggested that extraverts have a higher demand for sensory stimulation. The normal range of sensory stimulation found in everyday life may, therefore, represent a state of deprivation, or relatively greater state of deprivation, for the extrovert. The prediction that sport, since it provides many diverse forms of stimulation, will contain greater inherent reinforcing potential for extraverts rather than introverts, is logical and the evidence that extraversion is common amongst sportsmen is supportive.

Eysenck has speculated over the biological background of the extraversion-introversion continuum and has reached the following conclusion. In simplified form, the ascending reticular formation of the brainstem has a remarkable degree of control over the degree and intensity with which we experience our environment. It may serve to both heighten our perception of those stimuli arriving at us or inhibit the transmission of these stimuli to cortical levels. Eysenck suggests that there exist individual differences in the degree of facilitation or inhibition which this formation imposes, on average, on incoming sensory information. He contends that extraverts inhibit a greater amount of this stimulation and require greater degrees or intensity of stimulation in order to satisfy themselves. The introvert on the other hand may inhibit less of the incoming sensory information and in so doing find that there is a tendency for the environment to be overstimulating. He may, therefore, seek out those situations in which the intensity of stimulation is lower. Essentially the extravert is reinforced by an acceptable level of stimulation when involving himself in rapidly changing and intensely stimulating environments, whereas the introvert may be reinforced for those behaviours which lead to a quieter environment by achieving the same acceptable level of stimulation.

The influence of this physiologically-based individual difference on participation in sport is immediately obvious. The extreme introvert is likely to find most sports behaviours are overstimulating and therefore his failure to participate in sport may be predicted, whereas the extreme extravert may indulge in intensely stimulating sports because those activities provide this form of reinforcement.It has been stressed that personality, when viewed in these terms, must be thought of as a continuum and the extremes regarded as relatively rare. It is important to note that those who are not at the extremes may still be influenced to a remarkable extent by their degree of extraversion, not in terms of participation or non-participation, but in the kinds of sport which they choose. It is the lay impression, and probably quite an accurate one, that rugger players differ from long distance runners, team game participants differ from those who indulge in individual sports. These differences in the average personalities which participate in sports may be seen as a function partly of differences in reinforcement provided through inherent stimulation in these sports.

There is an additional factor in this context which may be made explicit. We have noted that there are inherent punishing stimuli within a number of sports. One cannot play soccer or rugger without bumps or bruises. For a given intensity of stimulation of this kind, it is probable that the introvert has a subjective impression of greater intensity of stimulation than does the extravert. In other words, the punishments provided by sport may be of greater influence on the behaviour of the introvert than on the behaviour of the extravert. We should expect to find that punishment will cause more rapid termination of responding on the part of the introverts because of this fact.

One demonstration of this link between punishment and its effects on introverts has been made in the skill of swimming. Persistant non-swimmers were found to be more introverted than the average population of children. The argument was made that the situation in which children learn to swim may have aversive qualities which become associated with emotional side-effects, particularly fear. The greater potential for conditioning in the introvert, since any given level of stimulation represents an effectively more intense stimulus for him, resulted in those children failing to acquire that particular skill.

Other researchers in personality have used different approaches to Eysenck's factor analytic study of personality. Instead of identifying three basic continua some researchers have extended the number, the most common being the sixteen personality factor test of Cattell (1965). Using similar techniques of measurement, the Cattell instrument enables the comparison of individuals on sixteen different factors, some being regarded as more important than others. In this way, personality profiles may be compared. It is apparent from studies using this test, that similar findings concerning the influence of personality types on participation in sport occur as in the case of Eysenck's studies. It is also apparent that the kind of sport an individual succeeds in is influenced in this way. Kane (1972) summarizes this phenomenon in the following way:

> These reviews tend to give a personality description of the male athlete or physically gifted individual in terms of extravert tendencies (such as dominance, social aggression, leadership, tough-mindedness) and general emotional control reflected in such trait measurements as low anxiety and high confidence. Women athletes are most often described as being like the men athletes on the extraversion dimension but being unlike them in showing a lower level of emotional control. There are, of course many exceptions to these general descriptions which have been reported and no doubt both the nature of the physical activity or sport in question and the subject's level of participation will in some way be reflected in characteristic ways of behaving. When the activity and level of participation are held constant interesting consistencies in personality have been demonstrated and evidence presented in support of the existence of certain sports 'types'. . .

The additional point which Kane makes in this summary is important. The personality of the top level performer in a particular sport may be different from that of lower level performers. The demands of participation and the reinforcements available for participation change as the level of skill and competition change. If we simplify for the sake of simplicity, we might argue that aggressive behaviour is an important component in some sports in the higher levels of competition. Aggressive behaviour will therefore receive reinforcement. Those who produce aggressive behaviour may receive greater reinforcement than those who do not. If aggression is essential for supremacy only those who produce this behaviour may reach the upper levels of that sport. Those who do not may have their participation reinforced for other aspects of their behaviour. If a personality survey is conducted we are likely to find greater levels of aggressiveness amongst those in the upper level of the sport. What we do not know, of course, is the degree to which the aggressive behaviour increases as a function of the reinforcement or how the reinforcement interacts with inherited tendencies to be aggressive or the degree to which prior reinforcement for aggressive behaviour generalizes to this new situation.

In behavioural terms those people with particular personality types are likely to find reinforcement in certain sports and not in others. The complete behavioural analysis has not yet been made and must eventually consist of relating the personality types to the history of reinforcement contingencies. In other words, what is it in the individual's past which has made him behave more aggressively than another? Individual differences in personality may have some basis in genetic differences. This seems to be implied in Eysenck's speculation concerning the physiological background of extraversion and introversion, but the modifiability of the individual through his experience is not known. It is an assumption of a behaviouristic approach that the conception of personality as a structure of internal traits will eventually be redundant and those behaviours which we classify as representing particular personality types, will be accountable on the basis of that individual's reinforcement history. In this way an additional step backwards in the causal chain may be made.

The same observations apply when other theories of personality are considered with respect to sport. A relevant example is the sensory-tonic field theory which began as a theory of perception but has subsequently achieved importance as a theory of personality. Using this approach, personality is scaled along a continuum from field-dependence to field-independence. Various testing systems have been developed which measure the degree of field-dependence and field-independence. Witkin et al (1962) suggested that field-dependent people are those who depend on their surroundings for their orientation, whereas the field-independent people are more internally directed and orientate themselves on the basis of inner direction rather than on external cues. A number of personality traits have been found to correlate with the degree of field-dependence-independence and there has been speculation that this description of personality or perceptual-style may have relevance to participation in sport. Kane (1972) argues that a field-independent individual should have less difficulty in acquiring those skills where perception of the body's position in space is of paramount importance, such as high-board diving or gymnastics. On the other hand, where the reaction of the individual to changes in his environment (where he is facing an opponent, for example) is more significant, the field-dependent individual may be at an advantage. In behavioural terms the field-independent individual is likely to find reinforcement in those sports for which that trait is an appropriate prerequisite. He will generally fail to be reinforced in the other sports and therefore his participation should eventually extinguish.

In terms of a behavioural analysis, this must be regarded as an interim conceptualization. It must be assumed that those aspects of behaviour which are labelled as showing field-dependence are the product either of innate factors or the result of learning. Supposing that the characteristics we label as field-dependent or independent are behaviours that are learned, those environmental contingencies which produce one rather than the other in an individual should be capable of description. We may still use labels to catergorize individuals, but the labels will then have causal explanation in terms of antecedent events. Personality will no longer be an unaccountable part of autonomous man, but will be subject to the same kinds of analysis as other aspects of behaviour.

Skinner himself is directly opposed to the kind of speculation which is outlined here. In a conversation with Evans (1968) Skinner made the point that he has always objected to 'filling in the gap' between behaviour and the independent variables of which it is a function with speculative theories. He is quite content that the physiologist may one day indeed fill that gap, but claims that this has little bearing on any current behavioural analysis.

Summary
In this section we have been mainly concerned with those factors which lead to non-participation in sport. We have considered extinction, punishment, omission training and various predispositions which are either genetically determined or are the result of the history of reinforcement. In the first section we reviewed some of the explanatory fictions which are used in the description of participation. This section has, I hope, questioned the explanatory fictions concerning non-participation. For example, failing to participate in sport because one has become 'discouraged' is no explanation, it merely means that extinction has occurred because no reinforcement has been supplied. A 'loss of motivation' usually refers to exactly the same process, but may be a legitimate explanation if it refers to states of deprivation. A lack of 'interest' in the sport and a poor 'attitude' toward sport may all be attributed to the consequences of the sports behaviour and it is this kind of explanation which is fruitful in terms of the manipulation of behaviour.

Section Four   A Behavioural View of Skill Acquisition

Introduction
One characteristic of all sports is that they require gross physical movement. Any further generalization is difficult to make. It is not even possible to suggest that all sports require the acquisition of a skill, since there are sports, such as running sprints or distances, in which the skill element is largely an overlearned aspect of the organism's repertoire before he begins the sport. (Distance running is perhaps the better example, since the sprint start can be regarded as a learned aspect of that sport.) Despite the fact that some sports require the learning of very few new movements, the majority of sports do require the learning of physical skills and this may constitute a major part of the sport. It is justifiable that we spend a section considering the mechanisms by which skills are acquired. In this section we shall consider learning from the point of view of the sportsman. Our concern here is with the mechanisms of acquisition and an attempt at a behavioural analysis of those mechanisms. Whereas in the last sections we discussed the question of the determinants of sports participation, we must now review the acquisition process in some detail, applying the same kinds of principles to the fine structure of skill.

Continuity in Behaviour
When an individual acquires any physical skill, he goes through a process of gradual differentation of movements, until he reaches the point where, under the appropriate stimulus conditions, only the skilled response occurs. We label that skill by its lay term; a baseball swing, a high-board dive, a high-jump. These acts are the end product of the differentiation process. The process of differentiation and shaping is often forgotten and we tend to view these behaviours as discrete units. In 1953 Skinner emphasized the continuity of behaviour in his book *Science and Human Behaviour.* His emphasis appears to have been neglected to some extent and yet the issue is of great relevance to sport.

A young child may be said to produce an undifferentiated set of behaviours. The process of producing a normal adult range of behaviour is one of gradual modification by the application of reinforcements. From the undifferentiated behavioural pool we select slightly unusual behaviours which, in a vague way, approximate some adult behaviour and reinforce them. The obvious example is that of language. The undifferentiated vocalizations of the infant are selectively reinforced by the parents. Any sound which resembles a real word is reinforced with social expressions of approval and affection. The child eventually learns the language. The same is true for motor behaviour; reinforcement is given for those responses which approximate the adult behaviour and closer and closer approaches are required before reinforcement is given, until the appropriate behaviour is acquired. In all of these differentiations we can see a continuity of behaviour in which greater and greater refinement is required until the final stage is reached.

When skill is examined in this way, it tends to ignore maturational aspects of behaviour. This is simply for the sake of simplicity and the two points of view are not incompatible. The evidence concerning maturation shows incontrovertibly that some motor behaviours are not susceptible to the effects of reinforcement until a particular stage of development is reached. When the child has matured sufficiently, the principles of reinforcement may then be applied. This process is an underlying genetic contribution upon which the acquisition of the skill is based. The tendency to implicate internal and unresolvable causes for behaviour has, perhaps, led to a greater level of importance being attached to maturational factors. If we take one example it will clarify the point. Many developmental texts suggest that walking is a maturational skill to which the principles of learning do not apply. It is suggested that the capacity to walk simply matures with age. The evidence for this comes, in part, from studies of swaddled children who are not allowed to exercise for periods of up to a year. It is argued that, since these children show no retardation in walking once the swaddling clothes are removed, the behaviour must be the result of maturation. If we analyze the situation more closely it appears that this is not necessarily the case. A child who is swaddled is still capable of observation. That is, the behaviour of walking in others may be observed. We have already noted that a generalized tendency to imitate the behaviour of adults may be reinforced in children. When the swaddling clothes are removed the child may produce this imitative behaviour and be reinforced for it by adults. Evidence from feral children, whilst often of dubious quality, may be cited in this context. If walking is a maturational skill in which learning or the impact of the environment has no part, why should it be that children raised by wolves run on all fours? There is additional evidence from children locked away in attics without social contact that walking behaviour does not simply mature. Presumably, there is an interaction between maturation and learning. The acquisition process, through reinforcement, must still be accounted as an important factor. This leads to a second point concerning the nature of the influence reinforcement. When a behaviour is emitted by an organism and that response receives reinforcement, there may be a drastic and immediate change in the frequency of responding. The negatively accelerated learning curve is frequently a function of an averaging process over a number of subjects. Any individual may show large increases in the probability of emitting a behaviour following a single reinforcement. To suggest that a behaviour cannot be learned or modified by experience, simply because it is acquired quickly, is to fail to understand the influence of reinforcement. The rapidity with which swaddled children acquire walking is perhaps more indicative of successful operant conditioning than of a maturational process.

It is true that physical skills appear to be acquired more quickly as the child matures. This is the result of two interrelated aspects. As the organism matures, the repertoire of potential behaviour increases. That is, the maturation process enables a child to produce more behaviours. (Notice that this is not to suggest that the behaviour itself matures, merely that its potential develops.) Simultaneously, the range of reinforcers under which the control of the child's behaviour may be brought, increases. As the child matures, many stimuli develop reinforcing capacities. The range of reinforcement which can be used with the child increases and the power of secondary reinforcers increases as a function of learning.

This aspect of learning is often neglected by educators and trainers alike. Secondary reinforcers are developed through experience of the environment. If a child does not appear to acquire a skill quickly, it is tempting to blame maturation, since this 'cause' of poor performance exonerates both the trainer and trainee. However, it is possible that part of the reason for failure is simply the inadequacy of the reinforcements used and the failure is not due to maturation entirely. A typical example of this fallacy occurs in terms of reading. It is often noted that 'reading readiness' occurs at around age six. It is said that when a child reaches this age he has matured sufficiently to acquire this skill. This statement may be regarded as accurate only if the proviso is made that readiness occurs at this age using current techniques of training. Alternative reinforcement contingencies may change the age at which a child is 'ready' for reading. The same argument may be used in terms of sports' skills.

It is often pointed out that the rate at which skills are acquired also decreases with age. It appears that while it may not be impossible, it becomes increasingly difficult to 'teach an old dog new tricks.' The actual empirical evidence for this assertion is very scant in sports. It should be possible to test the assertion experimentally; to try for example to train a group of children and a group of adults to ski using controlled instructional techniques. There are few, if any, examples of this kind of experiment with respect to performance in sports. The observation appears to be anecdotally based. One could suggest that the reports of coaches to this effect may be a reflection of their adequacy in providing reinforcers for the behaviour of these two groups. The reinforcer of adult approval may have a greater significance for a child than for another adult. Rather than being a result of maturation or a genetically determined reduction in the capacity to learn skills with age, differences in reinforcing capacity may be the answer. Two additional points need to be made in this regard. The comparison of adult and child novices may not be legitimate for a number of skills. Perhaps the observation could be made that adults are more difficult to teach to swim than children. In this case, we are comparing two unlike groups, in the sense that the children are presumably a random selection, whereas the adults are selected people who failed to learn to swim as children. Their failure to learn to swim previously means that they are a relatively homogeneous group; those with, for example, only low levels of the underlying abilities necessary for the sport, or, perhaps, of personality unsuitable to the acquisition of this kind of sport. In making our comparison, therefore, in which we find a significant superiority of the younger group, we should not be able to attribute this to an age difference *per se*. We have also noted previously that many sports contain inherently punishing stimuli. The magnitude of the punishment may be very much greater for the adult than for the child. With increased size, weight and momentum any fall, for example, is likely to result in far less injury to the child than to the adult. It is probable, therefore, that the adult will experience greater aversive stimulation consequent upon participation in a number of sports. So-called difficulty in acquisition may be no more than a reflection of this.

It is only on top of these considerations that we could look for evidence of decreasing capacity simply as a function of age. This may occur as a product of decreasing flexibility or other physical changes during adult life. Where there are specific physical demands which can be demonstrated to show deterioration during life, it is permissible to account for age differences in capacity by reference to maturational phenomena. For the most part, it seems that age differences are best thought of as supplying only a rough base of potentiality, upon which reinforcement contingencies may act.

The concept of continuity in behaviour is not restricted to refining and differentiation of responses with age. We can observe continuity of behaviour in terms of performance on a number of skills which show some degree of similarity. We referred to the concept of stimulus and response generalization in the first chapter and this is a related concept. Stimulus generalization is usually demonstrated by presenting a new stimulus similar to the one present when a response was acquired. The strength of response with that stimulus is then measured by some means. Usually the response is not reinforced in this test for generalization, since this would contaminate the stimulus generalization measure by creating a new acquisition process. In real-life situations, this response to new stimuli *may be* reinforced and acquisition begin to occur. The acquisition process is, however, much abbreviated, since some measure of response strength is brought to the new task. Response generalization is a similar process. An organism acquires several variations of a response while only one is reinforced. One of these responses, previously acquired through reinforcement in one situation, may receive reinforcement in a new situation. There is, therefore, a continuity of behaviour. Skinner (1953) points out very clearly that this conception of continuity in behaviour emphasizes that we arbitrarily label a unit of behaviour as a particular skill and tend to ignore the fact that the unit is by no means discrete and the label is merely for convenience. We should not be surprised to find so-called transfer of training occurring in the acquisition of skills. It is simply a function of this continuity of behaviour.

This kind of analysis also enables a reformulation of traditional theories of transfer. Instead of regarding transfer as a product of the fact that two skills possess identical elements, it is more accurate to say that the elements are strengthened whenever they receive reinforcement. If one total unit of behaviour, arbitrarily called tennis, is in fact a series of elements which have been strengthened through reinforcement, it should be no surprise to find that in

73

a situation where the stimuli are very similar, such as badminton or squash, many of these responses are made and also receive reinforcement. Our analysis of transfer of training is, therefore, quite simple. In Skinner's (1953) words:

> This leads us to identify the element rather than the response as the unit of behaviour. It is a sort of behavioural atom, which may never appear by itself upon any single occasion but is the essential ingredient or component of all observed instances. The reinforcement of a response increases the probability of all responses containing the same elements.

The same sort of analysis can be made with respect to negative transfer. Occasionally we find that the acquisition of one skill causes a reduction in the rate at which another is acquired. If we compare a group which has learned the previous skill with one which has not, and we find the latter learning the new skill more quickly, we suggest that negative transfer has occurred. If we consider the reinforcement of elements or 'behavioural atoms' which constitute the skill, the explanation of negative transfer is equally straightforward. If, in the new skill, similar stimuli are presented to those under which certain responses have been previously reinforced, then those responses are likely to be repeated. If these responses are not reinforced in the new situation, there extinction will occur. The appropriate responses for the new stimuli will be acquired as they are reinforced. This process of extinguishing one set of responses and acquiring another is likely to be more time consuming than acquisition alone. Because we tend to identify the skill as the unit of behaviour, transfer of training poses a problem to be explained. This problem is removed if we remain aware of continuity in behaviour and bear in mind that the labels we give to certain acts are somewhat arbitrary and the elements of those acts can be regarded as the units of behaviour with far greater justification.

The amount of transfer, in whichever direction, may be very difficult to predict. In changing from one skill to another, some elements of the response may continue to find reinforcement, whereas others may have to be extinguished. In sports skills, as opposed to highly simplified laboratory tasks, we are likely to find that both negative and positive transfer occur with reference to different 'atoms' of two sports. Many elements may be common to both of the responses, but some generalizations may be inappropriate.

There are other variables which will also influence this process. The degree to which a skill has been learned will determine the strength of the response 'atoms.' If one element, amongst others, has been reinforced over a long period of time, it will be very resistant to extinction, therefore increasing that component of negative transfer. Conversely, it will greatly facilitate the acquisition of the new skill if it is an appropriate response.

One aspect of stimulus generalization is important with respect to the acquisition of new skills and level of previous learning. When an old response has been made to a specific stimulus, similar new stimuli will serve to produce that response. However, the degree of generalization depends on the degree to which

74

discrimination has been reinforced in the past. If discrimination with respect to the stimulus has been reinforced, the degree of generalization is likely to be extremely small. An example will serve to illustrate the point. If a skill is acquired in which response X is reinforced to stimulus A, then when A_1 or A_2 (similar stimuli) are presented in the context of a new skill, generalization should occur and response X will be emitted. However, if in the original skill response X is reinforced to stimulus A, but in that same skill A_1 and A_2 are also present and the response X is not reinforced to these stimuli, the subject learns to discriminate and the tendency to respond to A_1 and A_2 is extinguished; there will be no generalization. Prior opportunity to acquire discrimination between stimuli through reinforcement results in a narrowing of the spread of generalization. There is also an interaction in this context with the degree to which a skill is learned. Where the skill is well-learned, it is likely that the extinction of inappropriate generalized responses will be relatively complete, but if only a low level of acquisition has been achieved, the extinction of generalized responses may not have been accomplished entirely.

Our analysis of transfer of training is dependent, therefore, on two interrelated concepts. The identical elements within two skills and the degree of generalization are equally important and both of these interact with the extent of previous learning.

One aspect of transfer of training does not lend itself easily to a Skinnerian analysis. There is a large body of evidence which shows that positive transfer of skill will occur from one hand to another. This phenomenon has become known as bilateral transfer. According to our above analysis, bilateral transfer should be negative, but is in fact positive. The stimuli in the situations are identical but the responses are different, since different hands are used. The tendency to make the initial response should, therefore, be extinguished first and then the new response acquired. The fact that positive transfer occurs in this situation must be attributed to a particular form of response generalization. In learning a task with the right hand, the process of shaping and reinforcement eventually results in perfect responding. During this process the subject has also acquired a tendency to make responses which are similar in some way to the acquired response. Performing the response with the left hand can be regarded as a similar response in this context.

The Acquisition Process
Feedback

When a new skill is acquired the generalization process and the continuity of behaviour have been justifiably emphasized. New elements of behaviour must also be acquired. It is these new aspects of behaviour to which we shall now direct our attention. In order for reinforcement to operate upon the behaviour there are two important prerequisites. The first of these is feedback. An organism must receive information concerning its behaviour:

The organism must be stimulated by the consequences of its behaviour if

75

conditioning is to take place. In learning to wiggle one's ears, for example, it is necessary to know when the ears move if responses which produce movement are to be strengthened in comparison with responses which do not (Skinner, 1953).

This stimulation may be provided to the organism through the exteroceptors; eyes, ears and skin particularly, but may also occur through the proprioceptors; feedback from muscles, tendons and joints. In our example, one may gain the appropriate exteroceptive feedback by observing the ears in a mirror, or, conversely, feel the ears move because of proprioceptive feedback. In lay terms we should say that the organism must know what it did in order for the reinforcement to be effective. Since Skinner's book in 1953 a great deal of research in operant conditioning has occurred and the implication of the preceding quotation that the organism must be able to consciously appreciate or 'know when. . .' it is stimulated, has been shown to be untrue. Many studies have now been reported in which the subjects are not consciously aware of the feedback, but the responses from which the feedback is derived may still be strengthened using reinforcement techniques. For example, Hefferline and various associates have conditioned small muscular responses. In one experiment (Hefferline, et al., 1959) they used a minute twitch of one of the muscles of the thumb, which after conditioning and extinction proved unnoticed by the subjects. They used an avoidance conditioning system in which the thumb twitch caused the termination of a loud tone imposed over background music. After the conditioning and extinction of this muscular response, subjects were unable to report what response had been effective in terminating the noxious state. Although we must emphasize the importance of feedback, this need not be construed as indicating that conscious awareness of the feedback is necessary. Indeed, much of the proprioceptive stimulation produced by movement is processed at levels below the cortex, notably within the cerebellum.

The feedback provided to the organism in the form of stimulation from its own activity may also perform the additional function of providing reinforcement. In our earlier discussion of participation, it was pointed out that there are inherent reinforcers and punishers in sports behaviour which are likely to determine, in part, the extent of participation. The same point can be made with respect to the fine structure of movement in the acquisition process. In acquiring a new move on the horizontal bar in gymnastics, for example, the learner may strike his legs on the bar in a painful way. The stimulation is both feedback from the response and also punishment. In the same way the stimulation from producing a behaviour which is appropriate for the sport may constitute both feedback and reinforcement.

This form of reinforcement may be delivered either via the proprioceptors or exteroceptors. The success involved in producing accurate responses which we can see may be reinforcing, just as the success associated with the 'feel' of an appropriate response may be reinforcing. For a large number of sports skills the stimulation provided through more than one modality may reinforce the response simultaneously.

Very frequently there is a temporal delay in the presentation of inherent reinforcers and punishers. For example, if we make a particular response in skating which results in a fall, that response may be said to receive punishment. However, the punishment in this case occurs after the response has been made. Although consequent upon the response, the painful stimulation produced by the fall is not part of the feedback from the response itself. The same is true for positive reinforcement. When a batsman produces a well-timed shot which carries the ball to the boundary, the feedback derived from the movement itself is proprioceptive and perhaps visual in the sense that he sees his own movements. After the movement is completed the sight of the ball heading for the boundary may be regarded as the subsequent reinforcement for that stroke.

One aspect of the relationship between feedback and reinforcement is the acquisition of a secondary reinforcing capacity by the feedback stimuli. This phenomenon tends to confuse an exact delimitation of what constitutes feedback stimulation and what is reinforcing. It will be remembered from section one that any stimulus which is frequently associated with a primary or strong secondary reinforcer will develop reinforcing characteristics. If a particular set of proprioceptive stimuli have been frequently associated with success they are likely to become reinforcing to the organism. The cricket example can be used as an illustration. The proprioceptive and tactile feedback associated with a 'sweet' shot, have been associated with the success of having the ball travel long distances in the past. The length of travel is reinforcing for the batsman. This reinforcement is likely to be of the strong secondary variety. It may be further reinforced by approval of team-mates and applause from the spectators. The fact that the proprioceptive and tactile stimuli are associated with strong secondary reinforcers on numerous occasions is likely to mean that they will, themselves, acquire reinforcing properties. Anyone who has played cricket will testify to the fact that, subjectively, the 'sweet shot' feels good and right. 'I didn't need to watch the ball, I knew it was a six as soon as I hit it.' This sort of remark is typical of the verbal accounts of the process we have described. The same sort of remarks are constantly made in a wide variety of sports. The reinforcing capacity of subsequent and consequent stimuli upon completion of the perfect response become largely redundant when the performer is receiving reinforcement from the feedback of the movement itself. One is equally aware that a specific response is wrong. If the response has frequently suffered punishment in the past, we are likely to find that the aversive consequences, being associated over time with the feedback from the response, acquire aversive characteristics. The anecdotal account of the perfect shot has its counterpart when punishment has been applied to a specific response. 'I knew it was wrong, as soon as I did it.'

The advantage of the inherent contingencies of reinforcement and punishment available in the acquisition of skill is that they are presented immediately.

When we discussed reinforcement and punishment in the abstract, it was emphasized that any delay in the presentation of these stimuli would result in a decrease in their effectiveness. The inherent reinforcers in skill are presented immediately and therefore have great influence upon the response. Those responses which are reinforced tend to become a part of the repertoire within the skill and those responses which are punished tend to drop out of the repertoire within the skill. This is a simplification of the process, since it ignores the question of stimulus control. Any response which is punished, when made in the presence of one stimulus may find reinforcement in the presence of another. This is important in the context of most sports. The response is not removed from the organism's repertoire by punishment, because it finds reinforcement in another situation, but becomes more restricted in its incidence of occurrence because of the differential consequences.

Not all inappropriate responses receive punishment. Many simply fail to be reinforced. This may then be regarded as an extinction schedule and the response in the presence of specific stimuli may eventually disappear because of the absence of reinforcement. If an alternative response under the same stimuli receives reinforcement, the situation is more closely analogous to counterconditioning. But many responses may simply be extraneous or superfluous to the skill and their production gradually ceases. One aspect of the effects of reinforcement needs to be clarified at this point. Reinforcement influences the strength of a preceding response. Very frequently the relationship between the two events is causal in nature, but this is not essential for reinforcement to have its effect. We have said that the visual stimulus of a cricket ball heading for the boundary is reinforcing and it makes more probable the response which preceded it under the stimulus conditions obtaining at that time. However, the reinforcement is likely to have an effect on the whole of the preceding response, whether some of the component parts were involved in the mechanical production of the flight of the ball or not. If we take a simple example it will clarify the point. If a tennis player bounces a ball twice before making his serve and the visual stimuli consequent upon the production of that response are reinforcing, then the influence of the reinforcement is upon the total response, including, perhaps, the bouncing of the ball.

Skinner has called this phenomenon the 'superstition' of organisms and the development of superstitious behaviour can be demonstrated in the laboratory. If a hungry pigeon is reinforced on a random basis with food, its behaviour is likely to become highly stereotyped:

> When food is first given, the pigeon will be behaving in some way — if only standing still — and conditioning will take place. It is then more probable that the same behaviour will be in progress when food is given again. If this proved to be the case, the 'operant' will be further strengthened. If not, some other behaviour will be strengthened. Eventually a given bit of behaviour reaches a frequency at which it is often reinforced. It then becomes a permanent part of the repertoire of the bird, even though the

food has been given by a clock which is unrelated to the bird's behaviour (Skinner, 1953).

The coincidence of a response and reinforcement when a causal relationship does not exist is still influential on the behaviour. Skinner argues that many human superstitions have their origins in these kinds of coincidences.

In sports the phenomenon is very common in the superflous mannerisms of performers. The behaviour of bouncing the tennis ball in a particular way, or straightening one's cap, before facing a bowler at cricket, or a particular shuffling step before taking a dead-ball kick in soccer are all mannerisms which bear no functional relationship to the consequences of action. These are bits of behaviour which, since they do not receive reinforcement directly, we should predict would extinguish. The fact that they are permanent reflects the fact that they are part of the total response and receive the reinforcement of the total response, even though they may not have 'caused' the reinforcement at all.

Generally speaking the idiosyncracies of non-functional aspects of the skill are unimportant in the determination of level of skill, but this may not be the case in terms of the elements of a total response. If an individual is performing a response which in total receives reinforcement, all the elements of that response will be strengthened. If one element is inappropriate or not optimum it will be strengthened also and be difficult to eradicate. If a high jumper produces a perfect straddle, but tends to bend the knee of the trailing leg, he may still find reinforcement in the sport, but a limitation is therefore placed on his performance. The 'bad habit' is difficult to remove since the inherent reinforcement for the total response is positive.

Knowledge of Results

This problem introduces a new factor in the acquisition process. If an inappropriate response is produced and the total response still receives some reinforcement an additional agency may be used in the modification of behaviour. The teacher, trainer or coach may supply new contingencies of reinforcement and punishment which are additional to the inherent reinforcers in the skill. As we have pointed out, the contingencies supplied through this process may parallel those inherent in the skill and in fact serve to establish the reinforcing characteristics of the inherent stimuli. For example, the coach who exclaims 'good, well done!' after a high board dive has thereby provided reinforcement for a specific set of movements and those proprioceptive stimuli associated with the movement will eventually acquire reinforcing characteristics themselves. The coach will also attempt to eradicate those components of the response which are less than optimal. It is in this context that a conflict is likely to arise between the reinforcements provided inherently and those produced extraneously by the coach. The relative strengths of these reinforcements is liable to determine the outcome of the conflicts. The difficulty of the coach in this situation has been stressed many times. Where the inherent stimuli have acquired secondary reinforcing characteristics and a component of the response is inappropriate, any change in the response is likely to 'feel wrong' to the participant. The reinforcers provided by the coach for the new response or punishment for the occurence of the old component must be very compelling for a lasting change to occur. Barbara Knapp (1963) quoted the following anecdote which is illustrative. 'A story used to be told of a swimmer who always swam with a certain part of his anatomy out of the water. Telling him had no effect and a catapult had to be used to convince him!' Provided that the new component becomes a part of the skill, through its reinforcement by the coach and the punishment of the inappropriate response, it will eventually develop its own reinforcing potential. That part of the response will come to 'feel good.'

During the acquisition phase the coach's primary function is the presentation of reinforcement for the performer. He is the instrument through which the shaping process occurs. The initial phases of skill are characterised by inappropriate responses to stimuli, by over and underestimation of the force of movements and by an inability to link successive series of movements together. The verbal knowledge of results supplied by the coach is a major contribution to the process of successive approximation to the final skill.

It is worth observing, parenthetically, that this relationship between the coach and the learner is symptomatic of an appreciation of deterministic principles. It is still common, however, for greater credit to be awarded to the individual who does not have this obvious form of control over his behaviour. The self-taught individual ('never had a lesson in my life!') whose behaviour is less obviously under the control of environmental contingencies, is still awarded greater prestige in society. Since the explicit environmental control exerted by a coach tends to be more efficient in the production of optimal behaviour, the self-taught individual is, perhaps, becoming a rarity, at least at the higher levels of skilled performance, but where he does appear this prestige still tends to be awarded.

Most frequently the coach is likely to present the performer with verbal reinforcement after the completion of a response or series of responses. Unlike the inherent reinforcers there is often a temporal delay in the presentation of reinforcement by the coach. This fact is likely to reduce the effectiveness of the reinforcement. It will make the alteration of behaviour difficult because the same component of a response may receive immediate inherent reinforcement and only subsequently punishment from the coach. As we noted in the first chapter, both reinforcement and punishment lose their effectiveness when any delay is introduced. For this reason many techniques have been derived which attempt to apply the reinforcement or punishment with less temporal lag.

One aspect of the interaction between coaches and their performers needs some explanation. We have talked so far of the coach issuing both verbal punishers and reinforcers to the athlete. These words may also contain information for the athlete which enable improvements to be made in performance. We can analyze the situation in a superficial way and suggest that there are two components to the coach's utterances — he gives both information and reinforcement. In this sense, the coach adds to the feedback which is inherent to the response. If a sprinter completes a training run of 100 metres the inherent feedback may indicate that he is running well. If the coach reports his time in seconds, he is thereby augmenting the feedback. The superficiality of this analysis is due to the fact that just as the inherent feedback may acquire reinforcing properties so may the augmented feedback provided by the coach. Therefore, it is usually not possible to identify two components but a complex interaction between feedback and reinforcement. Suppose, for example, the coach says 'Good, your time was eleven seconds,' it would be tempting to say that 'good' represented reinforcement and 'eleven seconds' represented augmented feedback. But if that time represented a new personal best for the performer, the information would also be very reinforcing. Producing a personal best time has been reinforced with social approval, praise and prestige in the past and is likely to have acquired reinforcing characteristics. The reinforcement or punishment provided by the coach in verbal form, may, therefore, simply take the form of information.

In many sports one of the functions of a coach is to make himself superfluous. He is attempting to produce skilled behaviour in the individual which will not demand the service of the coach at later stages. In other words, it is often the coach's job to provide augmented feedback which will later be unnecessary. In order to achieve this, the reinforcing aspects of the coach's comments must develop reinforcing characteristics in the inherent stimuli. The 'good, that's right' statement provides information to the performer and simultaneously reinforces him. When these stimuli are associated with the inherent stimuli of performance, the response should begin to 'feel right' to the performer. After this is achieved the coach's comments become redundant.

Normally, we find that variables influencing the reinforcing and feedback components of knowledge of results have similar results on responding. For example, increasing the amount of reinforcement is beneficial and increasing the amount of information concerning the response is beneficial. Also, in both cases, the value of increasing both of these variables produces diminishing returns. Just as increases in reinforcement produce successively smaller increases in response strength, so progressively increasing the detail of the information produces less and less additional improvement in the learning process. There is, however, one situation in which this parallel effect does not occur. We have noted that immediate reinforcement is superior to any delayed reinforcement in the shaping of behaviour. We have maintained that immediate reinforcement is automatic in terms of inherent stimuli and that immediate reinforcement from the coach is also desirable. Delay of inherent feedback also has a deleterious effect upon performance. In fact when delays in inherent feedback are artificially produced some skills become almost impossible. For example, if we speak into a tape-recorder's microphone and the tape-recorder records the words and feeds them back to us through headphones, but with a half-second delay, speaking becomes almost impossible. Delay of augmented feedback from the coach or trainer does not have the same impact and it may even be advantageous for some delay in providing this feedback to the performer. In an experiment by Annett

(1959) subjects had to learn to produce a particular pressure on a plunger. Some of the subjects received detailed information while they were pressing the plunger (immediate feedback), whereas others received information only after they had finished the trial. The group which had the immediate feedback learned to apply the correct pressure more quickly, but at a later stage in the experiment, when no information concerning the response was given to either group, there was a significant superiority for the group which had not received the information whilst in the process of applying the pressure. In this very artificial situation, giving continuous feedback proved a disadvantage for later performance. There is additional evidence that supports the view that delay of augmented knowledge of results does not necessarily retard the acquisition of a particular skill.

We have used the example of the coach providing knowledge of results in verbal form and it is probably true that in the majority of real-life situations this is the primary method. It is not the only method available and there is currently much experimentation in the provision of non-verbal knowledge of results. By and large these experiments have consisted of attempting to improve the informational component in the knowledge of results derived from sports skills. For example, in one of the earlier attempts in this direction, Howell (1956) used a force-time graph recording from a sprinter's foot as augmented feedback and showed a positive change in the performance of the skill. Increasingly, video-tape and film techniques are being used to fulfil the same function. These systems often serve to produce a separation of the reinforcing and informational components of knowledge of results, since the subject may be given verbal reinforcement, followed by technically presented information. This second component may then develop some reinforcing capacity.

Knapp (1963) pointed out that the coach of team games is often placed in the difficult situation of supplying knowledge of results to a large group of performers. Obviously, this is not an optimal situation since only the crudest survey of behaviour of large numbers can be made. The provision of technical aid in the provision of information is likely to be of greater benefit in this situation. Technical aids are also important, she points out, since they preclude the errors of observation which are likely on the part of the coach.

Many authors have suggested that knowledge of results are also instrumental in motivating individuals and providing incentive. Bilodeau (1966), Holding (1965) and Knapp (1963) all emphasized, in different ways, this supposed quality of knowledge of results. In the most technical of these descriptions, Bilodeau (1966) noted some doubts concerning this aspect. It seems probable that a motivational influence of knowledge of results has been added simply because of a tendency to attribute observable changes in performance to internal causes. Consider, for example, Holding's (1965) comments on this issue:

So far we have spoken only of the information value of knowledge of results. In fact it also appears to have a motivating function. Putting up day-by-day graphs of trainees' performance is a form of knowledge of results which may encourage them to better their efforts, or to compete with fellow trainees. . . . Several experimenters have noticed that people tend to lose interest in a task without knowledge of results.

The behaviours described by Holding are characteristic of the effects of reinforcement in the first place and extinction following the termination of reinforcement, in the second place. There is no need to involve motivational concepts in order to explain this behaviour, the concept of reinforcement is sufficient. Since we have limited our concept of motivation to the state of deprivation, it is not usually possible to use the concept in relation to knowledge of results and it would appear to be unnecessary. Holding admits the value of reinforcement but continues to invoke motivational concepts which are not entirely appropriate.

In one sense the informational and reinforcement issue in knowledge of results is not important. Much of the controversy arose from some of the pre-Skinnerian views of reinforcement. Under some of the theoretical analyses of reinforcement, it was common to relate reinforcement to internal drives and consider as reinforcers those stimuli which satisfied a particular drive. Where we use an operational definition and consider reinforcers only in terms of their consequences, information may be justifiably considered as a part of reinforcement since it does have an influence on preceding behaviour.

Attention

One of the most important aspects of acquiring many sports skills is the development of stimulus control of behaviour. The behaviour of the performer must be flexible to the demands of the situation. Earlier we had occasion to refer to Knapp's (1963) concept of a continuum of sport skills from those at the 'habit' end to those at the 'perceptual' end of the continuum. Where sports are concerned with the repetitive production of a single and relatively discrete set of responses, they lie at the habit end of this continuum. This is the case in the track and field events such as discus-throwing, shot-put, and high jump as well as other sports such as diving and gymnastics. The degree of stimulus control in these situations is relatively minor. In those sports in which strategy and reaction to an opponent is a central feature, stimulus control is likely to be of much greater importance. As we move along the continuum there are increasing demands made upon the performer in terms of his responsiveness to environmental stimuli. At the habit end of the continuum, where the movements of the skill are highly overlearned, this kind of responsiveness is not essential. One could suggest that the spring-board diver may respond to slight differences in the elasticity of a new board encountered in a competition or the discus-thrower may make slight adjustments in his technique if there is water on the throwing circle. In these kinds of cases reinforcement for the modification of the technique is provided by the quality of the performance and its consequences. Failure to make these modifications may result in punishment or the absence of reinforcement. With those sports at the perceptual end of the continuum there are far greater demands in terms of responses to the environment. What an opponent does, or what the teammates do, exerts fundamental control over the behaviour of the performer. In this context two issues are important. Firstly, the stimuli to which the subject responds must be familiar to him or at least sufficiently similar for generalization to occur and secondly, the subject must attend to the relevant stimuli. If he does attend and produces the appropriate response, he is likely to receive reinforcement. If he does not, punishment is likely to follow, or absence of reinforcement. During the acquisition phase of skill, much of the difficulty is due to the identification of the relevant stimuli to which responses of a particular kind receive reinforcement. It is through the process of differential reinforcement that finer and finer refinements to this aspect of the skill are made. Much of the seemingly miraculous feats of 'anticipation' by the highly skilled are no more than the identification on their part of controlling stimuli which are such a small part of the total environment that they go unobserved by the spectator.

It is part of the function of the coach to identify these stimuli for the performer and in this way reduce the time taken for inherent reinforcers to shape the skill. If a coach can point out that when a boxing opponent drops his left hand, he is about to make a right cross, the cue is effective since the appropriate response can be produced and the punishment consequent upon failing to identify this stimulus may be avoided. In more general terms, if a ball at cricket shows a particular flight path, or better still the bowler holds his arm in a particular way, these cues may be identified as stimuli signalling an off-break or leg-break. If this information is communicated to the novice by the coach, he is more likely to derive reinforcement from his subsequent behaviour. The process of bringing behaviour under the relevant stimulus control is therefore facilitated.

There are always an infinite number of stimuli impinging upon an organism at any given time. The limitations of the human organism are such that only a few of these may be attended to at one time. In order to carry out his activities man has to select those stimuli which are important and concentrate upon these while ignoring what is irrelevant to his current task. In achieving this there is a long acquisition process and one of the characteristics of the novice is his attempt to attend to too many features of the environment. He suffers from an 'information overload.' When the coach is able to reduce this overload by pointing out to the novice those stimuli which are important he enables a more rapid acquisition of the skill. A problem which arises in this context is the fact that many of the stimuli are internal and proprioceptive in nature. This means that there are seldom adequate verbal descriptions of the stimuli by which a coach could direct the learner's attention. The private sensations associated with movement are not readily communicable especially as much of the processing of the information appears to occur at sub-cortical levels. This restriction on the capacity of the coach is relatively greater in those sports which are at the habit end of the continuum, since a larger proportion of the relevant stimuli are likely to be proprioceptive. In these cases the technical systems of providing knowledge of results through such media as video-tape are highly significant assets since they provide a method of reflecting performance in which the internal stimuli associated with performance may be matched against their overt results.

In a behavioural analysis of sport it may be surprising to find space devoted to the concept of attention, since attending may not strictly be classified as behaviour:

> But if attention is not a form of behaviour, it does not follow that it is, therefore, outside the field of behaviour. Attention is a controlling *relation* – the relation between a response and a discriminative stimulus. When someone is paying attention he is under special control of a stimulus. We detect the relation most readily when receptors are conspicuously oriented, but this is not essential (Skinner, 1953).

Even where a stimulus is perceived in peripheral vision, for example, and an appropriate response is produced, we may remark that attention has been paid to that stimulus and the consequent behaviour is just as much under stimulus control as in the case of stimuli occupying the centre of the visual field.

At one point Adams (1966) noted that in analyses of attention:

> Many lean on the legacies of Guthrie and Hull that learning occurs to all stimuli impinging at the moment of response, but it is becoming increasingly clear that the human being is not a *tabula rasa* on which all stimuli write equally, and that the stimuli which the experimenter presents and manipulates for response may not enter totally into the S-R bond on each trial.

Unlike Guthrie or Hull a Skinnerian approach to attention does not imply that all stimuli are equipotential with respect to attention. Normally we pay attention to those stimuli consequent upon which reinforced responses have been made in the past:

> A sudden or strong stimulus may break through and 'attract' attention, .. (these stimuli) do so because they have been associated in the evolutionary history of the species or the personal history of the individual with important – e.g., dangerous – things. Less forceful stimuli attract attention only to the extent that they have figured in contingencies of reinforcement (Skinner, 1971).

We do not need to consider attention as a function of autonomous man in order to explain the phenomenon.

It is important that we also consider the alternative position. Why do people fail to 'pay attention.' When this problem is broached answers are frequently provided in terms of motivation. This is not, however, necessary. It is possible that situations in which an individual fails to make an appropriate response and then reports that this was due to lack of attention to a particular stimulus, are merely a result of two different aspects of the reinforcing process. In the first place, it is likely that there exists competition between stimuli in any game or sport situation. Sportsmen are reinforced for a large number of different attending responses. It is frequently the case that a selection of attending response has to be made and this selection may be in error at one point in time. 'Keep your eye on the ball,' is an instruction in directing attention. While this is heard with some regularity from coaching staffs, it reflects only one demand upon the attention of the learner. The reinforcements for following this instruction may, on average, result in optimum behaviour. But it is also an axiom of sport that one knows where one's opponents are and reinforcements may be given to this kind of attending response too. Under many conditions of a game these two demands may be compatible. When they are not compatible the selection of one attending response over another may produce failure. The soccer player who keeps his eye on the ball may be able to head the ball well (produce the appropriate response which has received reinforcement in the past) but the ball may go straight to a swift moving opponent to whom the header of the ball did not 'pay attention' and who placed himself cleverly for the interception. The alternative glance at the position of the opponent may result in failure in the accurate production of the response. The failure to attend may often be no more than the inaccurate direction of attention because of a history of reinforcement for a large number of different attending responses.

Whiting (1969) has also emphasized that the attending responses necessary during the acquisition phase of a sport may be quite different from those at later stages. For this reason the problems of identifying the relevant stimuli facing a coach are dependent upon the quality of the players in his charge. For example, it was noted in section three that for many skills there is a delegation of control from exteroceptive stimuli to proprioceptive as the skill level increases. Certain exteroceptive cues may be of great importance in the early stages of learning a skill. The performer who attends to these may be reinforced for his attending responses. At the later stages these movements may be controlled on the basis of proprioceptive information alone and attention may be directed elsewhere and reinforcement may be found for new attending relations. This process of temporal change in optimal attending responses may be under the control of the inherent reinforcers within the sport. Success in the sport may depend, for example, upon the learner's capacity to change his pattern of attending from exteroceptive cues associated with strategy, while maintaining the control of movements on the basis of proprioceptive stimuli. If this change is not accomplished the learner may fail to find reinforcement in the sport in total and the behaviour will extinguish. Very often the coach may attempt the direction of the player's attention to the important strategic exteroceptive stimuli. It may be a mark of the good coach that he knows the appropriate point in the development of the skill for this change in attentional emphasis to occur.

There is, of course, a difficulty in this transition. One set of attending relations has been developed by the novice on the basis of positive reinforcement. If progress in the skill is to be made, these now have to be changed. Sometimes this is difficult because the strength of the old response may be considerable and the disruption of skill caused by new responding, on the part of the learner, may result in a temporary reduction in the level of reinforcement. The example we used of the soccer player heading the ball is a case in point. To convert a soccer player from watching the ball all the way on to his head, to a technique of glancing at the position of opponents and teammates during the flight of the ball, is often a difficult response to establish. Yet this kind of adjustment may be essential to the achievement of an upper level of performance in the hierarchy of the skill. Verbal reinforcement and augmented knowledge of results provided by the coach form an interim reinforcement system which can serve to maintain the total behaviour until the reorganized response begins to derive inherent reinforcement.

At a more general level, when a player fails to attend to relevant stimuli this may be symptomatic of the general extinction of the total response. Paying attention is generally regarded as a function of interest in a particular event. In behavioural terms we may say that the completion of a task makes certain demands on an individual. If that response ceases to be reinforced, extinction of the total behaviour may occur. Aspects of the behaviour may extinguish at different rates and appropriate attending responses may extinguish more quickly than others. This process is likely to develop into a vicious circle in which the extinction of one aspect of the response produces lower levels of total reinforcement which, in turn, leads to an increased rate of extinction of other components.

Practice

Practice does not, of course, make perfect, but it is a prerequisite of perfection. In order to achieve the highest levels of skilled performance there are frequently lengthy periods of acquisition. The time spent on the sport may be correlated with level of performance but it is only a low level of correlation. Given the individual differences discussed in the last section this is not surprising, but even were individual differences to be held constant, length of practice would be unlikely to assume major importance on its own. What is far more significant is the quality of the reinforcing contingencies available during practice for components of the skill. Simply devoting time to the skill without differential reinforcement for appropriate versus inappropriate actions is likely to result in only minimal changes in the level of skill. These differential reinforcements may be most effectively provided by the coach, but this is not altogether essential. In some cases, the inherent reinforcers will provide the learner with the differential reinforcement necessary to achieve progress. In order for self-improvement to occur it is also necessary in many sports that the performer be self-critical and self-analytical. This suggests that the individual indulges in some form of self-control. Superficially this statement appears untenable in the light of our behaviourist orientation, yet it is a conception which is often stressed by writers on the topic of sports psychology. Knapp (1963) made the point in the following way:

> A person who wishes to learn on his own can do a great deal by intelligent self-testing and may indeed make fast progress through developing a highly sensitive appreciation of his own weaknesses and strengths. He must learn to check the results against his intentions. Thus a tennis player should not get satisfaction merely because he wins the point. If he serves an ace but the ball has gone nowhere near where he intended it to go then his skill is not good but bad and he should get no pleasure from it. Similarly in the case of a goal scored by a mis-kick or mis-hit no matter how much public acclaim the scorer may receive.

The fact that this is obviously true causes some problem for a behavioural analysis. It would appear from Miss Knapp's argument that control has passed from the environment to autonomous man. In other forms of behaviour it is customary to refer to this as control becoming 'internalized.' It is not essential that we regard self-control as a product of autonomous man, however, since we can trace a direct series of stages in conditioning which is environmentally based and which leads to this behaviour. This series of stages is based upon man's verbal behaviour. We can describe social contingencies of reinforcement and punishment which enable an individual to benefit from the experience of others. Generally speaking we are reinforced for following these verbal directives. To the extent that this occurs in sport, apparent self-control is achieved, yet autonomous man is not responsible, it is merely that the control processes are no longer visible. For example, the quotation from Knapp above is a part of this directive verbal behaviour. She contends that reinforcement is likely to follow the analytical behaviour she describes. This observation is based on many years of coaching experience. Those who follow her advice behave in a way which has been previously reinforced, i.e., doing as good coaches tell them. If an individual is able to derive his own rules from analysis of the contingencies, Skinner points out, the stages of control are even less evident and we tend to give credit to the performer for his behaviour.

Knapp's directive is that the performer ignore fortuitous reinforcement and accept only reinforcement which is a product of a causal relationship. The performer who accomplishes this is likely to achieve greater reinforcement in the future since, Miss Knapp argues, the procedure will lead to a greater level of reinforcement in the future. During the acquisition of a skill this is a frequent problem and also requires a distinction between behaviour during practice and during competition. Where an individual is in practice, those behaviours which will lead to an ultimate high level of reinforcement are those which are likely to be reinforced by the coach and, if the verbal conditioning has occurred, be directed by the performer himself. These may not constitute the best behaviours to employ in the competitive situation. In competition, reinforcement is provided immediately for current level of performance and the performer who produces his best available repertoire of responses is more likely to receive reinforcement, even though this set of responses may not be optimum for ultimate level of performance. An example will clarify this point. If a tennis player has a weak backhand stroke, ultimate level of performance will depend, in part, on his capacity to improve that stroke. If he fails to improve it his level of success may remain low. In practice, therefore, the coach is likely to direct and provide reinforcement and punishment for backhand shots. The performer who is under some measure of 'self-control' may have observed the contingencies associated with poor backhand play and direct himself to the practice of this stroke. On the other hand, when he is in competition, he may 'run around' his backhand in order to make his stronger forehand shot. He is playing the shot which is likely to result (in his experience) in a greater probability of reinforcement in the short-term. This analysis of the situation consists of an identification of differences in the long-term and short-term contingencies of reinforcement. When an individual or a coach identifies these differences, behaviour may be modified depending upon the situation, whether it is competitive or not.

Self-instruction requires that the individual is well acquainted with the sport in question. It is unlikely that the novice will know sufficient about the sport for his behaviour to be efficiently placed under this type of control. Once he has gained some of this experience, periods of time devoted to the development of self-instruction in the behaviour may have remarkable effects upon performance. This may be regarded as a speculative explanation of the reminiscence phenomenon. Sometimes, after a period without practice, a performer will produce a much improved level of skill. It is often difficult to attribute this improvement to the reinforcement of overt behaviour. During that interval of time, however, it is possible that the individual engages in extrapolating new rules for his behaviour on the basis of the experience of contingencies within the skill. This in turn may lead to a more coherent attempt at the skill subsequently. In this context we are identifying the controlling variable in the reminiscence phenomenon as mental practice. It has been suggested by a number of studies that mental practice facilitates the acquisition of skills. In our behavioural analysis we should say that the derivation of rules from experience of the contingencies of reinforcement and punishment in the sport may form the basis for improvement in skill on a subsequent occasion. Since the reports of studies vary with respect to the degree to which mental practice is facilitatory, we must conclude that there are different degrees to which this is possible depending on the skill, perhaps because generalized rules of performance may be more useful in one type of skill than another. Individuals are also likely to vary in the degree to which they have been reinforced for this kind of rule-identification behaviour in the past.

This observation leads us to a consideration of the conditions under which maximal improvement occurs as a result of practice. The literature of motor skill research is very confused regarding the influence of distribution of practice upon performance. In the light of our comments concerning mental practice this should not be so surprising. Individuals and skills differ in the degree to which an interval in the physical performance of the sport may be used to the benefit of that sport. There are also additional factors. The degree to which mental practice is valuable will depend on the level of skill of the performers. When we compare distribution of practice and its effects upon performance, therefore, it is probable that we are comparing skills which are not identical in their level of acquisition. Young (1954) made a similar point in acknowledging the fact that this may be the case where the skills are apparently new to the subjects, since different degrees of transfer of training may occur.

It is also likely that no single optimal schedule of practice will be identified because of the different physical demands made by skills. The influence of fatigue upon performance may be quite dramatic and serve to determine the schedule of practice to some extent. If a skill produces fatigue and fatigue is an aversive state then punishment is applied to long practice sessions which may influence not only the detailed structure of the skill, but may also have an effect on total participation. Usually this phenomenon is described in motivational terms but these are not necessary. It is frequently suggested that long practice sessions may have a deleterious impact on skill because the subject loses his motivation. Often this is not the case and the apparent inaction of the performer is due to the aversive consequences of massed practice. It is possible that in certain restricted situations a motivational explanation of massed practice is possible. In laboratory studies with animals it is conventional to ensure that they are constantly in a deprived state for the duration of the experiment. If they are being reinforced with food, for example, experimental sessions never last so long that the animal becomes satiated. In the complicated situations of real life it is possible that massed practice with consequent massing of reinforcement may result in satiation of the subject. Should this occur there may be a tendency to terminate behaviour with consequent loss in the strength of acquired responses. As we have seen, the reinforcements for sport are multifarious and the satiation may occur with respect to only one of the reinforcing stimuli. The impact may not necessarily be great, but is likely to be disruptive to the total acquisition pattern. For example we discussed the reinforcing potential of the novel stimulation produced by sport. This novelty may 'wear off,' that is, satiation may occur, and hence some of the reinforcement of the behaviour be lost.

In this context we are suggesting that massed practice is disadvantageous. However, it may have advantages over spaced or distributed practice as a function of retention. With the elapse of time low-probability responses in the repertoire may tend to either disappear or reoccur when appropriate stimuli are present, but in some modified form. The issue of memory has been dealt with very little by Skinnerians, mainly because it deals with unobservable internal processes. Skinner (1971) remarks at one point that:

> We say that a person *recalls* or *remembers* what he has seen or heard but all we see is that the present occasion evokes a response, possibly in weakened or altered form, acquired on another occasion. We may say that a person *associates* one word with another, but all we observe is that one

verbal stimulus evokes the response previously made to another. Rather than suppose that it is therefore autonomous man who ... recalls or remembers, and associates, we can put matters in good order simply by noting that these terms do not refer to forms of behaviour.

This dismissal of memory does not alter the fact that overt behaviour is, of course, subject to the influence of memory. The way in which the memory processes affect overt behaviour may be quite lawful and predictable and there is justification for research into the process, even though Skinner apparently does not feel that it is necessary as part of a behavioural analysis.

To return to our theme, it is probable that the elapse of time in distributed practice may cause higher levels of forgetting than massed practice. The fact that there is inconclusive and contradictory evidence concerning optimal distribution of practice in skill-learning is a reflection of these competing factors.

A similar degree of confusion exists concerning the superiority of whole or part methods of training, and for similar reasons. Many sports skills are extremely complex and some are extremely simple. There is little possibility that one or other method will prove optimum for all. Nevertheless, an examination of the issue does reveal some of the reasons behind the contradictory evidence. The reinforcement of parts of a complex skill, by a coach, may serve to maintain the behaviour when attempts at the whole skill would result in such lengthy sequences of failure that extinction of the behaviour would occur. This process may be unnecessary if the skill can be completed with some success from the outset. In this case splitting the skill into parts may reduce the reinforcing potential in the situation. Even where the skill is complex, attempts at the total skill may give some reinforcement where partial success is possible. Again, the factor of memory is likely to be important. Some loss or change in the characteristics of a response may occur when parts are practiced in discrete units. It is also probable that the coherence of the response components of the skill will be influential. To learn to serve at badminton and to practise this part is possibly advantageous. The serve is a relatively discrete unit. If we divide that serve into its subcomponents, this kind of practice may be extremely wasteful, since the coherence of the unit would be lost.

One of the major practical contributions of operant conditioning has been the application of its principles to classroom learning. Programmed instruction involves the division of material into parts which are acquired by students and receive immediate reinforcement of various kinds. Research continues to find better and more sophisticated methods of presenting the material and reinforcing the responses made by subjects. Some estimates are that effective techniques can halve the acquisition rate of some kinds of school material. The system of programmed instruction is not without critics, however, and any prolonged discussion of the principles is out of place here. The observation is made because it would appear to be far simpler to decide on whole versus part techniques of training in an academic setting than it is in the context of motor skills. A majority of skills do not lend themselves to a division into discrete progressive units which may be taught and reinforced independently of each other. This is particularly true of sport skills. The absence of literature related to programmed instruction for motor skills is both a reflection of this fact and a consequence of the reinforcement contingencies mentioned above.

Flexibility of Skill .

One of the most salient features of highly skilled performance in many sports is flexibility. Superior performers are able to change and adapt their behaviour to extremely variable conditions. This aspect of skill caused some problems for early behaviourist theories which relied on the development of S-R bonds for their explanation of learning. When the performer adapts his skill to new circumstances and maintains his level of skill despite disruptive influences, it is impossible to regard that behaviour as a rigid S-R habit. The flexibility of skill presents no such problem for a Skinnerian point of view. Flexibility of responding may be reinforced and punished in just the same way as other quantitative aspects of behaviour. We can examine this in terms of one example. In facing an opponent, the repetition of a stereotyped response to a given stimulus 'may be successful and hence receive reinforcement initially. After a time this repetition is likely to be punished by the opponent.The predictability of the performer is punished rather than the response itself. Suppose that each time a tennis player receives a serve to his forehand he attempts a cross-court shot. The shot itself may be perfect, but the fact that it is predictable is likely to cause punishment of the behaviour since the opponent is presented with a discrimina- tive cue with which to make his own response. On the other hand, selection from a variety of returns may receive reinforcement. It is neither constructive nor appropriate to think in terms of habits of responding and the term habit is only one step removed from the explanatory fiction of autonomous man. Where we have spoken of a 'habit' skill it is preferable to translate this in terms of reinforcement for a stereotyped pattern of behaviour. The topography of a specific response is subject to the influence of reinforcement. We may produce more forceful responses, gentler responses or faster responses depending on the degree to which they are reinforced. In those skills at the 'habit-end' of the continuum, there is reinforcement for a particular topography which leads to stereotyped behaviour. At the other end of the continuum, there is greater reinforcement for alterations in the topography of responses and this is revealed in the practices of the superior performers.

This interpretation of flexibility is also a component in a discussion of strategy. Frequently coaches talk of developing a 'sense of strategy' or talk of players with good 'tactical sense.' Both of these mentalistic conceptions are unnecessary. All we are able to observe is the behaviour of the individual in the game situation and his verbal reports of that behaviour. The fact that an individual produces a response which results in his own or the team's success is what is important.

When this response is made on the basis of obvious discriminative stimuli, we do not use the expression 'good strategy.' If the stimuli are less obvious and few players appear to have identified an appropriate stimulus, then we tend to apply that label. For example, if a soccer player receives the ball in front of his opponents' net with no one else around and scores a goal, we may applaud his skill, but not his strategy since the discriminative stimuli for that response are obvious to all. On the other hand, if a player makes a pass between opponents to a team-mate running in an unexpected direction which then results in a goal, we are likely to applaud the strategy involved in the pass. All we are saying is that the discriminative stimuli in that situation were less obvious to us as observers. The identification of controlling stimuli of these kinds is reinforced by the success of the consequent response. The 'sense of strategy' is no more than this. If the player is able to verbalize generalized rules concerning his behaviour and communicate these to others, then this behaviour may be appropriate in the modification of the responses of others. The team-game coach, for example, plays this role. When practice of various playing strategies occurs, the coach may predict on the basis of his experience what another team will do and have the team prepare responses in advance of the discriminative cue, or by having the situation simulated with 'dummy' opponents.

In some team games, North American football and baseball, for example, it is possible for the coach to 'call the plays' during an actual game. His 'strategic sense' is therefore of paramount importance and the players' capacity to detect and respond to relevant stimuli may be severely restricted.

In this context, the concept of deception is also important. When facing an opponent we are aware of the fact that we are presenting to him discriminative stimuli which are, in turn, cues for his responses. If these cues are very obvious the opponent has an advantage in selecting his appropriate response. If our behaviour provides few of these cues our probability of success against this opponent is therefore enhanced. Minimizing our production of discriminative cues of assistance to the opponent is reinforced with increased success. It is even more probable that we shall be reinforced if our behaviour produces false discriminative cues. If we can make movements which represent stimuli to the opponent which have previously been associated with one response and ourselves produce an alternative bit of behaviour which demands a different response on his part, his error is likely to result in greater reinforcement for us. The deception of opponents by the display of 'false' discriminative cues is a component of many sport skills. It will be noted that there are two distinct aspects of this behaviour. First, a response tendency in the presence of one discriminative stimulus must be developed in the opponent. Normally, this is transferred from previous experience. Through stimulus generalization the opponent is likely to produce a response in the presence of this new stimulus. If the tendency to respond is not transferred, it may be developed in the course of the game by the player. He may produce discriminative cues and make one response. Secondly, after the tendency has been developed by whatever means, the same discriminative stimulus can be presented and a different bit of behaviour may follow. The resulting error on the part of the opponent is then equivalent to a reinforcing success for the deceiver.

The two parts of the process of deception interlock. If the deceiver continues to produce his false discriminative stimulus the opponent's original response will extinguish and a new response will perhaps find reinforcement. Reinforcement for deception is therefore contingent upon its infrequent use. Just as in other social circumstances a known 'deceiver' may find his ploys no longer successful, so in sport skills deception does not receive reinforcement if it is predictable.

The question of deception is closely related to the perception of the environment. The deceived player perceives a stimulus complex and makes an inappropriate response. In other words he has responded 'as if' a stimulus had other properties. Skinner (1953) has referred to this as the 'interpreted' stimulus. He emphasizes that this is not a distinction in terms of 'real and unreal' aspects of the world:

> We operate in one world—the world of physics. Organisms are part of that world, and they react to it in many ways. Responses may be consistent with each other or inconsistent, but there is usually little difficulty in accounting for either case (Skinner, 1953).

Speed and Accuracy

Most texts concerned with the acquisition or teaching of skill find it necessary to comment on the question of speed and accuracy. In many everyday skills it is possible to make a trade-off between these two aspects of performance. We can, for example, type very quickly and make errors or type slowly and make few. In some sport skills this is also possible, but generalizations are difficult to make. What is of greater difficulty is the question of training. Should responses be learned at a slow rate with an emphasis on accuracy and speed be increased later, or should responses be produced at a fast rate and accuracy later, or should emphasis be placed on both components. If we examine the issue from the perspective of the skill and the learner first, the question of training procedure can be more easily resolved.

When a new response is acquired it is a product of the contingencies with which it has been associated. Fitts (1966) demonstrated very clearly that the reinforcement and punishment associated with the components of speed and accuracy determined the topography of the responses produced. In this experiment reinforcement and punishment were provided by giving and removing points for level of performance. The group which was highly rewarded for speed with only a low level of penalty for error, produced fast, relatively inaccurate responses. The group which received low reward for speed and high penalties for error were slower and more accurate. The available contingencies produced different topographies of responding. The problem in many sport-skill situations is that both speed and accuracy may be reinforced at different times and absence of speed or errors may be punished or not punished at different times. In other words, the contingencies are not consistent as they are in the experimental laboratory. If we take the example of the bowler at cricket, we can illustrate the point. His reinforcement or punishment is partly contingent upon the quality of the batsman who faces him. A fast ball which is inaccurate may be punished by the good batsmen, but may so intimidate the poor batsman that he makes subsequent errors, thereby reinforcing the bowler. Any particular inaccurate ball may be missed and therefore receive neither reinforcement nor punishment. Where the contingencies of reinforcement are inconsistent there is great difficulty in predicting the likely performance of the individual. Where the optimum performance of the individual is both speed and accuracy only the combination of both will inevitably result in reinforcement. If the punishment for slowness or inaccuracy is variable there are likely to be large variations between performers in the way in which their behaviour approaches this optimum.

The problem for the coach is, therefore, difficult. First of all he must assess the trade-off between contingencies of reinforcement and punishment within the skill. His reinforcement to the performer may then reflect these contingencies. For example, he may emphasize speed and reinforce speed and fail to punish verbally some inaccuracy or reinforce accurate responding to a smaller degree. In practice, therefore, the coach may reflect in his reinforcements and punishment the average contingencies in the sport itself. If a performer can 'get away' with occasional inaccuracy, but is more frequently heavily punished for this behaviour, the coach may well choose to insist on accuracy and reinforce it and verbally punish the inaccurate response.

Generalizations about the way in which the two components should be acquired are pointless in most cases. The question of speed or accuracy is entirely dependent upon the contingencies associated with these components in a specific skill. One generalization which is legitimate, however, is that where speed is a component of the final response, it should be reinforced initially since the acquisition process may result in an acquired topography of responding which must be relearnt if speed is increased.

Section Five   Social Phenomena in Sport

Introduction

There has developed over the last decades a distinct sub-discipline in psychology whose major concern has been the social behaviour of man. Social psychology is devoted to the elucidation of principles of behaviour of people as they interact together. To this end much of the work has dealt with such topics as aggression, competition, attitudes and communications between individuals in group settings. These aspects of social man's behaviour are of prime concern to those interested in sport. We have already considered some of the reinforcing and punishing potentialities of the social situation, but in this section it is intended that attention be devoted to some of the categories of social *behaviour* in sport and that a Skinnerian analysis of them be presented.

Competition and Cooperation

Whiting (1972) defined competition as being:

> . . . concerned with striving against others or against the natural environment in order to bring about some personal or group gain.

In a behavioural analysis it should first be pointed out that the intentionality implicit within the phrase is unnecessary since it makes intention a component of competition. When all we can observe is overt behaviour and it is this with which we are concerned, the definition may be simplified and made acceptable by suggesting that competition is striving against others or the natural environment. The second half of Whiting's definition is, in a sense, an attempt to explain the behaviour. According to the tenets of the behavioural system it would be more accurate to suggest that competitive behaviour is a product of the environmental contingencies of reinforcement and punishment with which it has been associated. Also, the idea of competition against the natural environment does not conform with a general understanding of the term. Normally, we talk only about competition between people. A behavioural definition of competition is more concerned with the consequences of behaviour:

> Two individuals come into competition when the behaviour of one can be reinforced only at the cost of the reinforcement of the other (Skinner, 1953).

The same definition would be applicable where two teams are involved.

This point of view implies that competitiveness is an acquired aspect of behaviour which is subject to the same principles of acquisition which govern those other aspects we have already discussed. The evidence for this contention is quite sound. Differences between cultures in the average degree of competitiveness exhibited indicate that competitiveness is culturally determined and susceptible to the social contingencies which control behaviour. Sutton-Smith (1961) has summarized some of these cultural differences in an examination of tribal cultures and their sports activities. He pointed out that not only do cultures differ in the degree of competitiveness of their sports but that some cultures apparently fail to produce competitiveness in sports at all. In the face of evidence of this kind we are led to assume that competition in sport is not a reflection of an innate tendency to compete but is rather the product of man's experience. In order to explain differences between cultures in their degree of competitiveness it would be necessary to examine their cultural history to determine the reinforcements which have been derived by the culture for this behaviour. Presumably the initial stimulation and consequent reinforced competitiveness may have resulted from an externally derived set of circumstances, which may or may not still be in existence. In Section two we mentioned the fact that although the original cause of an aspect of behaviour may have disappeared from the culture, the transmission of the behaviour to subsequent generations may occur as a product of cultural reinforcement for the verbal reinforcement of the behaviour. The competitive behaviour may, in other words, be perpetuated because people are rewarded when they reinforce competitiveness in others.

The fact that there exist differences between cultures in terms of their competitiveness in sport should not be surprising when the reinforcement contingencies are considered. Similarly, individual differences succumb to the same kind of analysis. Within our own culture, which exhibits a good deal of competition within sport, there exist wide individual differences in the degree to which people are competetive. In large measure these differences can be explained without reference to a concept of competitiveness at all. When an individual does not participate in sports it may be a function of punishment or lack of reinforcement with which that behaviour has been associated. To label his failure to participate as a lack of competitiveness is to provide an unnecessary explanation of the phenomenon in many cases. However, there may be situations in which the explanation has some validity. Where an individual has received reinforcement for competing against others in his previous experience, he may be more likely to continue to do so in sports behaviour than an individual who has not been reinforced in this way. If demonstrations of superiority over others have received reinforcement in general during childhood, for example, it is possible that a generalized tendency to demonstrate superiority is generated. In terms of sports participation, the performer with this generalized response tendency is more likely to pursue sports behaviour than one who has not.

Obviously the reinforcements which the individual has derived in the past are going to be important in determining his participation, but perhaps the kinds of sport in which an individual indulges are influenced to a greater extent. There are numerous examples of sports which do not involve competition between people, even though they may involve a struggle between man and his environment. The rock-climber, for example, is not generally regarded as a competitor. Some prestige may accrue because of one individual's superiority over others, but it seems unlikely that this is a significant aspect of the reinforcement for that particular sport. Those who have grown up with a lower level of reinforcement for competitiveness may find that the reinforcement for this kind of sport are more influential upon their behaviour than the reinforcements available through competition in others.

Although an explanation of different levels of competitiveness can be offered in terms of contingencies for this kind of behaviour, it may be that there exist predispositions toward competitiveness at a genetic level. Competitiveness is frequently regarded as an element or aspect of personality. As we mentioned in section three, the degree to which traits are a function of inherited or environmental determinants is not known. While postulating a genetic component in competitiveness is not necessary in explanatory terms, such an inherited factor may exist. The fact that some cultures do not show competitiveness indicates that in any event the genetic factor must be merely a predisposition which is inherited. At an anecdotal level there seems good evidence for the fact that children raised in similar environments may differ substantially in the degree to which they are competitive. This would seem to implicate a genetic factor although the strict behaviourist would point out that the environments of children are never identical and a fortuitous reinforcement of one action may have a profound effect upon later behaviour.

Despite these comments it is not fruitful to attribute competition to 'human nature.' The extreme modifiability of behaviour in its interaction with a currently unknown genetic basis for competitiveness is an indication of the importance of environmental factors. The fact that sport is generally competitive has been cited as a reflection of western culture. Because so much of western culture is dependent upon competition between individuals there is a temptation to trace in it the influence of autonomous man. This is true in the following quotation:

> Within a society that fosters personal gain through competition, and where competition is pursued as far as it is necessary, it is not surprising that man's *will* fosters a superman cult. Sport, as a mecca for man's competitive nature cannot suddenly become a palace for mutual sharing (Slusher, 1967).

Slusher's argument, that man is by nature competitive, is not acceptable in the light of cross cultural evidence. Simply because one category of behaviour, known as competitiveness, receives reinforcement in a number of different situations and hence becomes fairly typical of a culture, should not lead us to attribute that behaviour to autonomous man. The behaviour is still under environmental control. It is also probably correct that there is a 'spread of effect' in terms of competitiveness in society through the generalization process. It is not acceptable to cite this as evidence for the action of autonomous man either. Slusher is quite correct in suggesting that sport cannot 'suddenly become a palace for mutual sharing.' Where reinforcement is provided for competitiveness, there is no doubt that this kind of behaviour will continue, no matter what exhortations are made to the contrary, but this is the result of similar reinforcements in different situations not the product of 'man's nature.'

Many writers on the subject of sports' skills have referred to the fact that competition leads to the improvement of performance. An individual performing a task alone is likely to show a lower rate of improvement than one who performs with a group. This effect is often attributed to the motivating influence of competition between individuals but it may be regarded with equal validity as a reflection of environmental determinism. The fact that superiority in behaviour over others has led to reinforcement in the past, should lead a performer to select those responses which lead to superiority in the new situation. One could predict, for example, that if the same experiments concerning the facilitatory effects of competition were to be carried out in those societies in which Sutton-Smith (1961) found an absence of competitiveness, it would be found that no such facilitation occurred. Only where a generalized tendency to compete has been reinforced in the past, is it likely that facilitation of performance will result.

Frequently a contrast is made between competition and cooperation between individuals. This is implicit in the quotation from Slusher (1967). It is usually considered that the two types of behaviour are antithetical. Whereas western society is rightly referred to as highly competitive, it may also be labelled highly cooperative. Where people act in some form of unison we tend to call the behaviour cooperation and, obviously, in a society in which division of labour reaches the extremes currently found in western culture, much of man's complex behaviour must be thought of as cooperative. Though much of sport is competitive there are also cooperative aspects both inherent to a competitive framework and as a part of the total sport. The example of rock-climbing was used as an illustration of sports in which there is a lack of competition. It will also serve as an example of cooperation. Through a system of mutual help both members of the team derive the reinforcements available from that sport. Without this cooperation both punishment for the behaviour and failure to find reinforcement become more likely. The acquired nature of cooperativeness is easily demonstrated in infrahuman organisms and Skinner's many experiments on cooperation in pigeons are well known.

There is greater complexity in the study of cooperation in competitive situations. In team games it is tempting to say that a team which cooperates well is likely to maximize the probability of receiving reinforcement in its competition against another team. This is true and is a point which team-game coaches are at pains to stress. What is frequently forgotten, however, is that the

99

reinforcements for team-game participation are of two distinct types. There are those reinforcements available for the team as a whole, derivable through winning, but there are also those available to the individual for his own individual performance in the team. Frequently these reinforcing contingencies serve a parallel function. What is an appropriate response for the individual is appropriate for the team, but there are occasions when a response made by an individual is likely to increase the probability of individual reinforcement and reduce the probability of team reinforcement. The obvious example is that of the 'greedy' player who attempts a shot at goal when a better positioned colleague could have received a pass. The influence of a dual-reinforcement system can lead to this kind of behaviour. Sometimes this is partly a function of the competition which exists between team mates. It is an often ignored fact that team mates may regard each other as competitors for the limited number of places available on the team. In their experience individual brilliance has been reinforced by inclusion in the team. When encountering a new situation the influence of this reinforcement history may have considerably more impact on behaviour than the reinforcers provided for the performance of the team as a whole.

In this account of reinforcement for cooperation and competition we find an acceptable explanation for the behaviour which Slusher (1967) attributes to man's 'nature' in the quotation above. It is not that it lies against man's nature to cooperate, it is merely that the contingencies of reinforcement for competition have produced a greater tendency to produce this behaviour rather than cooperation. Where appropriate contingencies of reinforcement are so developed it is perfectly possible for cooperation to occur.

It should be stressed that there exists within team games a system of group control through the use of different varieties of punishment which adds to the complexity of the situation. Individual performances which lead to a failure to find reinforcement for the team may be punished verbally by team mates, but are also likely to result in the exclusion of the 'greedy' player. It is the balance of these influences which result in the team behaviour as we observe it.

Aggression

Aggressive behaviour is common in a large number of sports where it may constitute either a *raison d'etre* as in boxing or where it is a common, though perhaps an undesirable, side-effect as in the case in many body-contact team sports. Aggressive behaviour is difficult to define because the subtlety of man's behavioural repertoire provides him with the capacity to injure another in an infinite variety of ways. The degree of injury may vary from marginally 'hurt feelings' to death and yet the cause of the injury come under the same label. The degree to which the tendency to injure another in some way is genetically determined is not known. In examination of behaviour of infrahuman organisms it is apparent that a high proportion of intraspecies aggression is innately determined. Individual differences in man also give the superficial impression that degree of aggressiveness is related to innate factors. Nevertheless, it is also true that the aggressive behaviour of both man and animals is highly susceptible to modification through operant conditioning. For example, Baisinger and Roberts (1972) showed that even the 'reflexive' fighting of paired rats to the presentation of electric shock, may be manipulated by the use of reinforcement. On the basis of evidence of this kind it is impossible to regard the genetic component of aggression in man as providing any more than a potentiality upon which environmental contingencies may operate.

With respect to the nature versus nurture discussion regarding aggression, Skinner has made the following comment:

> Our way of life encourages it (aggression) because you often get what you want when you fly into a rage. People who annoy you then leave you alone. I suspect that it is an acquired response, because we are much more likely to get mad at people than at things. If you walk down a street and your way is blocked by several hippies who refuse to move, you may react with resentment and anger and say something to them if you dare. You may not attack them then and there, but may suggest passing a law to keep people from blocking the sidewalk. But if you go down a street and find that a tree has fallen across it, you walk around the tree and feel no tendency to aggressively attack. This suggests that we have acquired our angers because they have paid off. Getting angry at a tree is not often reinforced. If we can build a world in which rage doesn't pay off, it will be a world in which people don't fly into a rage at the slightest annoyance (Skinner, in Evans, 1968).

In examining the situation within sport, it is apparent that reinforcements are provided both overtly and covertly for aggressive behaviour. At one extreme there are the sports in which attempts to injure opponents are sanctioned by rules and superiority is, at least in part, dependent upon the performer's capacity to do this. The reinforcements contingent upon success in boxing are based on the capacity to injure another. The overt reinforcement is provided for this kind of behaviour. In team games of the body contact variety there is likely to exist a discrepancy between the environmental contingencies placed upon aggression. At the level of a performer selecting a response from his repertoire, those which have previously been reinforced with success are more likely to occur in the current situation. If aggressive behaviour falls into that category, it may be used even though alternatives are frequently available. Where there is conflict with the rules of the game, punishment is likely to follow. However, if punishment is not administered consistently it may not eradicate the behaviour and if aggression receives partial reinforcement with only intermittent punishment, it is unlikely to decrease in frequency. The coach who is in a position to extrapolate rules concerning the contingencies of reinforcement and punishment within the game-situation is also likely to come under the control of these factors. He may, therefore, reinforce illegal aggressive behaviour in his teams simply because, in his estimation, the probability of reinforcement for the team is greater than the probability of punishment or the derivable reinforcement outweighs the potential punishment.

In many cases, the value of aggressive behaviour is both obvious and sanctioned by the rules of the game, but it is also probable that the function of aggressive behaviour is more subtle. Punishment, as we have seen, is often associated with emotional responses such as fear. There is a tendency for escape or avoidance responses to be made in the presence of those stimuli which have been associated with punishment. This factor is important in the selection of aggressive behaviour. By punishing an opponent physically, it is possible to produce these effects on the other's behaviour, thereby facilitating future success against that opponent. In lay terms, aggressive behaviour intimidates the opposition. The success of this behaviour will determine its future use.

Both in the press and amongst physical educationists there has been discussion concerning aggression in sport and very frequently the phenomenon has been decried as 'unsporting.' Attempts have been made at encouraging coaches to stop this behaviour on the part of their players. The players themselves have been exhorted to show more 'self-control.' These attempts at the modification of behaviour are obviously inept when the reinforcers for the aggression remain unchanged. Public censure through the media may be regarded as punishment for aggressive behaviour, but at most it is inconsistent and unlikely to have much effect for that reason. It is also more than counter-balanced by the simultaneous reinforcement for the behaviour from many other segments of the community and from the success which which the behaviour tends to be associated.

An additional cause of the failure of punishment generated by the media to influence behaviour on the field is its temporal relation to the offence. The effectiveness of punishment is always markedly reduced when any delay is introduced in its presentation. The press provide their censure the next day, whereas the reinforcement for the aggression is immediate. The influence of such delayed punishment is probably minimal. The same point may be made for fines or suspensions levied some time after the act by controlling authorities.

There are obvious cultural differences in the reinforcement provided for aggressive behaviour. This is reflected in sport in a distinct difference between the reinforcement provided for males and females in their aggression. Western society, as a whole, tends to reinforce aggression in males to a very much greater extent than in females. In parallel fashion, western society also tends to punish females for aggressive behaviour to a much greater extent. That aggression is more common in male sports is determined by the fact that not only are greater reinforcements available to men within that context, but also the males are likely to have a longer experience of receiving reinforcements for aggression in many different contexts. The male has probably found that aggression is reinforced in many situations and he will have a much greater tendency to react aggressively in a new situation. For example, boys are much more likely to be verbally reinforced for reacting aggressively to any aggressive behaviour directed at them than are girls. Any stimulus in the sports context which is perceived as

102

being aggressive is likely to stimulate aggression as a reaction. Within our culture there are also class differences in the degree to which aggressive behaviour is condoned. The lower classes tend to reinforce aggressive behaviour, in general, to a greater extent than the upper classes. This is again likely to influence the degree to which any individual will produce aggressive behaviour in sports contexts.

Finally, it is necessary to mention the large collection of research evidence concerning aggression and imitative behaviour. In observing aggressive behaviour in children many studies have reported the imitation of aggressive behaviour when apparently little or no reinforcement is available at the time. For example, if a child is placed alone in a room with dolls after watching a film of a model behaving aggressively towards such dolls, he is likely to produce the same kinds of responses. The observation can be made that the child has a history, as we all have, of reinforcement for imitative behaviour. In terms of sport this may be a significant factor. When children observe aggressive behaviour in sport they are likely to produce the same kind of behaviour themselves in that situation out of a generalized tendency to imitate. Even when there is no clear reason for belief that in a particular instance the behaviour will be reinforced, the aggressive behaviour is likely to occur simply because the child has observed it before. One of the findings from research in this field is that the prestige or status of the model is an important determinant of the degree of imitation. In sport the superior performers are credited with very high status. Their behaviour is likely to be imitated to a greater extent for this reason, and where it includes aggressive activity, we should not be surprised to find that these actions are also copied by children.

One of the common views of aggression in sport (and to a lesser of competition) is that it has some cathartic value; that by engaging in aggressive sports we rid ourselves of 'pent-up' aggressive emotions. Such an analysis is both unnecessary and also misleading. The behaviours can be adequately explained in terms of their consequences, as we have seen. It is misleading in the sense that such an assumption leads to misdirected attempts in the control of such behaviour. If we wish to modify aggression in sport the 'pent-up' emotion explanation would direct our attention to the individual's experience outside sport and to relieving those situations which produce his 'pent-up' state when entering sport. The behavioural analysis directs our attention to the consequences of the behaviour in the sport itself. By changing the contingencies of reinforcement, aggressive behaviour can be manipulated. Even when a performer brings to his sport generalized tendencies to respond aggressively, by such manipulation we may eradicate those responses through the processes of extinction, punishment and omission training. In order to achieve such manipulation we must take into account all, or a very large proportion of the reinforcers which are available and produce such behaviour. A simple alteration of rules within the sport may not be sufficient if verbal reinforcers and prestige remain as consequences. When the reinforcers have been identified the behaviour can be altered.

Social Facilitation

A majority of sports are conducted, at some stage, in a social setting. Even the 'loneliness of the long-distance runner' changes when he indulges in competition. The public performance of sport skill has an effect on performance. It is a frequent observation that the quality of performance will be changed by the presence of a group of observers. This is typified by the statements we make about performers. The athlete who can produce his outstanding performances on the 'big occasion' is an obvious example. There has been a good deal of research into the influence of onlookers on various kinds of behaviour and the area of research has become known as social facilitation. This research has produced a complicated picture of the interaction between a performer, his quality of behaviour and the onlooker. At first it was thought that the presence of onlookers always led to an increased level of performance and it was this observation which gave the field of research its name. However, recent experiments have led to a far more complex view of the interaction. Zajonc (1965) demonstrated that the presence of an audience will produce inferior performance early in the acquisition process whereas it will produce superior performances at later stages. This finding has been replicated a number of times. Notably Martens (1969) showed that this transition in audience effects occurred in the performance of complex motor tasks.

In a Skinnerian analysis this finding is rather difficult to explain and requires that we concern ourselves with influences on behaviour of various emotional states. The presence of an audience may be thought of as a reinforcing or punishing situation, depending upon the level of skill. Any performer entering a skill learning situation in which an audience is present will do so after long experience of performance in front of others. Failure in front of such an audience may have led to punishment, either verbal or in terms of loss of prestige. Success will have led to positive reinforcement. Associated with each of these contingencies there may occur emotional responses. The emotional response in association with punishment may be called fear. Stimuli such as audiences may therefore lead to a tendency to produce avoidance responses and a result of this may be the poorer selection of responses by the organism for the skill at hand. Performance is likely to enter a vicious circle in which failure is accompanied by emotional responses which are associated with punishment. This, in turn, produces greater probability of avoidance or escape responses and hence failure and consequently greater punishment. A novice may, therefore, be influenced adversely by the presence of an audience. When an experienced performer is placed in the same situation, a reverse effect may be predicted. The probability of success for the experienced performer is greater and an audience can be regarded as a potential source of yet higher levels of reinforcement, with a consequent influence upon level of performance. The fact that the transition from novice to superior performer ever occurs in front of an audience is superficially surprising. The vicious circle effect that we pointed out with respect to the novice would seem to preclude this development of skill. However, it must be remembered that the audience is not the only source of reinforcement within the skill learning situation. There are likely to be inherent reinforcers which will serve to counteract punishments available in the situation. Added to which any appropriate response by the individual, even though a novice, may receive counterbalancing reinforcement from the audience.

This explanation differs markedly from social facilitation theory which is essentially based on drive theory. A drive interpretation suggested by Zajonc (1965) postulates arousal as an intervening variable. An audience is said to increase level of arousal, which increases the performer's generalized drive state, which in turn produces a tendency for an organism to emit dominant responses. Since the dominant responses tend to be incorrect during the initial stages of learning, the relatively slow rate of acquisition by those whose performance occurs in front of an audience is therefore explained. These two views of audience influences are not incompatible, it is merely that a drive theory explanation attempts a detailed hypothetical description of the associated emotional responses and attributes different behaviours to their influence.

Attitudes Toward Sport

A considerable proportion of research effort in social psychology has been directed toward establishing effective methods of measuring attitudes and theorizing over the mechanisms of attitude change. There have been attempts to provide scales for the measurement of attitudes towards physical education and sport. From these studies it has been frequently reported that participation in sport and attitude towards sport are correlated. Those who like sport indulge in it and those who do not, fail to participate. This kind of result is neither surprising nor should it be considered particularly significant. This result achieves significance when attitudes are considered as a reflection of autonomous man and not simply a second-hand observation of behaviour. When it is suggested that some inner man has these 'attitudes' and these cause or determine his behaviour, the implications may have considerable adverse effects on the treatment of behaviour. It is frequently averred, for example, that if only we could change teen-age girls' attitudes towards sport, we should find a great increase in participation. It is further considered that the creation of a 'good attitude' toward sport and activity is a fundamental role of the physical education teacher, since this will lead the student to participate throughout life.

These points of view are both erroneous and also lead to an extraordinary misdirection of effort. The root cause of the error lies in the misunderstanding of the nature of what is measured in an attitude scale. Attitude scales normally attempt to sample two components of behaviour and their associated emotions. Since it would be inconvenient to measure these in a real-life context, they are measured using a paper and pencil test. The components are thoughts about the topic and overt behaviours with respect to the topic. From a summation of positive and negative values given in answer to these questions a final score is derived. If we consider the case of sport, it is quite simple to develop questions which provide evidence concerning each of these components. If someone has a negative attitude toward sport it simply means that he fails to participate or fails to enjoy participation or thinks that sport is a poor way to spend his time. His answers to the questionnaire may be regarded as one set of responses. If we now measure another kind of response, his overt participation, and find it fairly infrequent, we should not be surprised. When we find a consistent correlation between responding on a paper and pencil test and responding in real life we may claim to have discovered a Response-Response or R-R law of behaviour. The correlation does not, however, indicate causality in either direction. Suggesting that the teen-ager does not participate in sport *because* he has a poor attitude toward sport is saying no more than that he fails to participate because he fails to participate and is meaningless.

Attempts to modify behaviour by modifying attitudes are not likely to be successful. What is needed in this situation is an understanding of how these two sets of behaviours have been developed. Why is it that our subject has developed a tendency to give negative verbal evaluations of sport and also fail to participate? The contention made here is that the question is already answered in our sections on the reinforcements, punishments and other contingencies which surround sport. If an individual has been punished for a particular bit of behaviour, we have seen that there are likely to be negative emotional side effects and responding is likely to be reduced. If we require this individual to make a verbal report, it will also be negative. Where positive reinforcement has been provided we should anticipate increased participation, positive emotional response and also positive verbal reports. In effect, therefore, the root of causality lies in the antecedent contingencies of reinforcement and not in the correlations between behaviours. The misrepresentation of attitudes as indicants of a quality possessed by autonomous man rather than another aspect of behaviour lead to inappropriate manipulations.

Stable attitudes tend to be formed by puberty and to remain relatively consistent thereafter. However, attitudes along with any other learned aspect of behaviour are subject to modification. If an individual has acquired one set of responses both verbal and physical, these may be modified by a change in the consequences which follow them. The classic attitude change studies conducted by Newcomb (1943) at Bennington fall into this category. A marked change was noted in the degree of students' liberalism during their time at this liberal institution. It was concluded that peer group approval and social acceptance reinforced verbal espousing of liberal ideals. The relatively conservative freshmen developed a liberal set of verbal behaviours under these circumstances. In terms of sports behaviour the same analysis may be applied without difficulty. Where an individual expresses through his verbal reports a dislike for sport, a modification in the contingencies of reinforcement concerning sport participation may produce considerable change. All components of behaviour subsumed under the heading of attitude to sport may be modified in this way. In other words, we may reinforce those statements which are positive when they occur or extinguish or verbally punish those statements which reveal a negative evaluation of sport. Simultaneously, we can reinforce any tendency to participate. With sufficient positive reinforcement, behaviour will be modified and a positive emotional response will become associated with it.

There is evidence which suggests that it may be unnecessary to influence each component of the total behaviour which we label as an attitude. Numerous studies have reported on the phenomenon of cognitive dissonance in which it is demonstrated that inconsistencies in behaviour tend to be eliminated. Presumably our societal structure reinforces consistency in behaviour. We tend to apply punishing verbal labels to people who do not show this consistency. We call them hypocrites. The fact is that if by means of reinforcement an individual begins to participate in sport, the verbal reports are likely to change fairly rapidly too. The discrepancies between behaviours are likely to disappear since consistency of behaviour has tended to receive reinforcement in the past.

Achievement Motivation

Another of the concepts frequently used in social psychology and relevant to sport is achievement motivation. A large body of evidence has accumulated on the relationship between levels of success in diverse activities and this form of motivation. The concept is far removed from a Skinnerian use of the term motivation, since it does not seem to imply any state of deprivation. The concept of achievement motivation found its major impetus in the work of McClelland and his co-workers (McClelland, 1961). He suggested that individuals vary in the degree to which they have a need to achieve. The strength of this particular need determines the strength of the motive to achieve in a large variety of circumstances. In assessing achievement motivation, McClelland developed a test in which subjects are required to write short stories concerning briefly presented pictures. The stories are then analyzed for the degree to which they reveal need for achievement.

Significant correlations have been found between these test scores and the kinds of achievements demonstrated in real life. For example, a higher proportion of highly achievement-motivated individuals occupy entrepreneurial positions than those with low levels of achievement motivation. McClelland has also demonstrated that there are significant cultural differences in mean levels of achievement motivation which he has related to the material success of those cultures.

Using this concept gives us superficially satisfying explanations of behaviour, particularly in the realm of sport. When we are asked why an individual strives so hard to achieve excellence in his chosen field, it is apparently explanatory to suggest that having given him a test we find he has high achievement motivation and it is because of this that he works so hard. The problem again lies with the word *because*. We have attributed causality to a correlation between two sets of behaviours—one is the test behaviour and the other the real-life behaviour. This assumed causality is given a veneer of validity by the assumption that the paper and pencil test measures some attribute of autonomous man. We believe we have measured some internal characteristic which causes the behaviour. What is needed, of course, is a knowledge of those antecedent variables which have resulted in these two sets of behaviour and, to some extent, researchers into achievement motivation have attempted to identify these. McClelland has demonstrated that child rearing patterns are salient contributors to achievement motivation. He has shown, for example, that children who are rewarded for independent behaviour, and, provided this does not imply rejection by the parents, are punished for dependency behaviour, are those who develop high achievement motivation. When these kinds of variables are identified the concept of achievement motivation becomes essentially redundant. It is no longer necessary to conceptualize autonomous man as possessing a 'need to achieve.' Instead we explain current behaviour both on paper and pencil tests and in real-life situations on the basis of the contingencies of reinforcement which have occurred in that individual's past. The internal man does not have a need which he satisfies but an individual's behaviour is under the control of preceding events. It is they which have produced generalized tendencies to be determined, to compete, to strive and to take risks.

One may argue that since the influential variables have been delineated there is no reason not to accept a simple unifying label and agree that the concept of achievement motivation refers to a set of related tendencies to respond. However, the continued use of the term serves to misdirect efforts at the modification of behaviour. In order to increase generalized tendencies to produce those behaviours which have greater probability of leading to achievement, we should be concerned with manipulating the appropriate environmental consequences of the subject's behaviour. A conception of the phenomenon involving motivation or internal need would lead to efforts to raise that level of motivation perhaps by deprivation of achievement or some other such manipulation which is inappropriate.

In his discussion with Evans (1968), Skinner confronted this issue and made the following comment:

> As to achievement, however, people generally tend to overlook the extraordinary importance of the conditions of reinforcement. The important thing is not that you are getting something; it is what you are doing at the moment you get it. I could make a pigeon a high achiever by reinforcing it on a proper schedule. I can't do it by ordering the needs. I don't know how to order needs.

One result of the view that achievement motivation is an attribute of autonomous man is the surprise that is felt when people show different levels of striving towards success or achievement. Recently Zander (1974) expressed this surprise in distinguishing between group and individual achievement motivation. His experiments and those of his co-workers demonstrated that individuals may work hard to achieve success for a group when they may not have been scored as possessing high achievement motivation at an individual level. This evidence is perfectly understandable when we analyze it in behavioural terms. In his experience of the contingencies of reinforcement in the past, an individual may have discovered differential forms of reinforcement for personal and group success. This has led to, perhaps, entirely different tendencies to respond when presented with a new group or individual situation. In spite of this parsimonious explanation of differences, Zander (1974) sees some fundamental differences between the group and the individual setting:

> The main difference between group achievement motivation and individual achievement motivation lies in our assumption that the desire for group success is not a permanent trait of individuals, but rather a motive that develops in particular situations (Zander, 1974).

The view could be reinterpreted by suggesting that the only difference is a temporal one. Individual striving for success has received a relatively consistent form of reinforcement in the past, whereas group success has received more variable consequences. Hence behaviour in the group is subject to the more immediate contingencies whereas individual behaviour tends to be more persistent. We do not need to assume any permanent internal 'trait' to account for the discrepancies in behaviour. In spite of the non-behavioural approach which Zander (1974) takes, his conclusion is essentially a Skinnerian solution:

> By creating conditions that nourish group desire for success and then by rewarding group accomplishments, I believe many of our institutions could become more flexible and more involving for a larger part of our population.

In other words, by manipulating the environment and producing appropriate reinforcers, desired behaviours in groups can be achieved. Using this analysis the concept of a group achievement motivation would seem to serve relatively little purpose. No doubt much of what is called team spirit, *esprit de corps* or group motivation can be examined in this way.

Creativity in Sport

One of the common criticisms of Skinner is that control of behaviour will lead to uniformity; that a designed culture will inhibit creativity. There is a superficial validity in this criticism. If reinforcing contingencies are identical for everyone a tendency toward stereotyped responding is likely to result. However, some variability in responding is a distinct feature of the operant conditioning procedure. If this were not the case shaping of behaviour through the process of reinforcing successive approximations would not be possible. It is only because a conditioned response shows some fluctuation in topography that this procedure is possible. From this standpoint a culture with planned reinforcement contingencies would not show stereotyped behaviour in an exact sense. In addition to this observation we can also note that variability of responding may also be manipulable by reinforcement. In terms of the design of a culture, there is likely to be not a single optimal behaviour, but rather a range of behaviours

109

which are acceptable. It is within this range that variability may be encouraged through reinforcement. Besides this it may be found that the genetic differences between individuals will provide sufficient variability to prevent the development of a society of stereotyped automata.

When the term creativity is used it normally refers to an aspect of behaviour which is something more than simple variability in topography. In fact creativity is frequently viewed as a prime attribute of autonomous man. We tend to think of great artists or composers containing within themselves a well or spring of entirely new or novel actions. This is our explanation because we cannot identify the kinds of controls which the environment has exerted over their behaviour. It is perhaps more honest to state that we cannot really even identify the behaviours in any coherent way and perhaps this is the major problem. If it were possible to define exactly what is meant by a creative behaviour we would be in better position to determine or at least guess at those factors which produce them.

In sport, creativity is used as a descriptive term in many situations. We may talk about a creative player, by which we tend to mean one whose actions are not predictable on the basis of our experience. He is the player who tends to be successful by finding novel methods of achieving particular objectives. This analysis of the situation renders it amenable to a behavioural interpretation. Doing the unexpected is a form of responding which can be reinforced and manipulated. Studies of conformity have tended to show that we can be pressured in group situations into behaving as other people are behaving. We receive group acceptance as reinforcement for this conformity. More to the point in this context is the fact that if an experimenter reinforces deviations from conforming behaviour, these deviations will increase. That is, conformity or deviation from group norms of behaviour can be manipulated.

It is probable that deviations from norms of behaviour may frequently receive such reinforcement in sport. The novel and surprising bit of behaviour on the part of a player may 'pay off.' In competitive situations, the stimulus of a person performing in some new way has not been associated with reinforcement or punishment in the past, even through the process of stimulus generalization. The opponent has not acquired any specific tendency to respond within such a situation. It is, therefore, likely that a novel method of performing may prove initially successful and novelty itself be reinforced.

This is only one interpretation of the meaning of the word 'creative.' It can also be interpreted to mean some artistic quality in performance. This is usually the case in the context of those sports in which some aesthetic judgement is made concerning the quality of responding. For example in high board diving, women's gymnastics or figure skating, the qualitative aspects of performance are taken into account in deciding success or failure. There is no easily definable set of responses which can be reinforced in this situation. This is not a limitation on reinforcement theory but is, to a greater extent, a limitation on the capacity to describe the behaviour accurately. Grosser characteristics of suitable responding may be describable but beyond this the task becomes difficult. For example, pointing one's toes when the foot is off the ground appears to be compulsory for aesthetic reasons in gymnastics. This bit of behaviour can be trained. In figure skating, however, the judges' marks for artistic interpretation seem to involve a judge in acquiring an overall impression of the performance, reacting to very subtle aspects such as fluidity and total grace, rather then to specifics. Where this is the case, the training of the performer according to operant principles is far more difficult. We must assume that the trainers and performers are themselves unaware, in precise terms, of what responses they are trying to achieve. Behaviour may be supposed to consist of relatively random attempts and modifications until the coach finally agrees that the performance 'looks right.' The behaviour may then become stereotyped through reinforced practice until competition. The verbalization of what constitutes the appropriate quality of responding never occurs and the granting or withholding of reinforcement by the judges in competition is what eventually decides the value of the coach's or competitor's behaviour.

The mystique which surrounds the word creative has developed because of our inability to prescribe those behaviours which we label as being creative. This leads to a tendency to credit autonomous man with the capacity to be creative. Nowhere is this more true than in Adler's (1927) view of the existence of a 'creative self.' Adler suggested that the creative self interprets life and creates fulfilling experiences. It is only when we remove this conception of man and begin to analyze the behaviours that we can make progress in causing people to be more 'creative.'

In considering the question of originality in a much broader context the reinforcement of creativity in behaviour is not a sensible goal. In order for any order to exist within a culture a degree of conformity is essential and useful. Reinforcing novelty for its own sake is of little value:

> The important creative steps which mean something to people are, of course, applauded; we don't know how to encourage creativity except to applaud it when it occurs. But although people are prepared to accept a certain kind of novelty, and reinforce the men who achieve it, they are not usually prepared to accept, and in fact are disturbed by, anything which is very different (Skinner, in Evans, 1968).

Section Six   Implications of a Behavioural Analysis

Introduction

In the course of this book an attempt has been made at analyzing the phenomenon of sport from a Skinnerian point of view. Skinner attempted this kind of analysis with respect to a culture in *Beyond Freedom and Dignity* and in his earlier writings, his view of man and his prescriptions for change were met with criticisms. Perhaps this will be the case with the view presented here. However, the analysis has been made and it leads to some prescriptions for changes in the treatment of sport in society. Before examining some of these changes, it is defensible that we consider some of the criticisms which have been made concerning Skinner's views in the current context.

One point which is frequently developed by critics is that they feel they would not enjoy a society in which there were planned contingencies of reinforcement. The apparent removal of 'freedom of choice' would not be emotionally satisfactory. This argument is based on two misconceptions. It implies there is currently some 'choice' available and that planned contingencies would remove this choice. Those who promulgate this kind of view have apparently partially accepted the deterministic view. They are accepting the contention that man can be controlled, but appear to believe that he is not currently controlled. The essential concept to understand is that behaviour is currently the product of inadequately planned contingencies. The problems in behaviour are problems that have arisen, not because of freedom of choice, but because of inadequacies in the controls that are currently exercised. Considering this point in the context of sport, we could argue that the failure of many people to participate in sport is not the product of their freedom of choice, but is a result of inadequate use of the reinforcers available for participation.   The second misconception is that a planned and controlled society is necessarily aversive:

> There are, of course, good reasons why the control of human behaviour is resisted. The commonest techniques are aversive, and some sort of counter control is to be expected (Skinner, 1971).

Those who fear control tend to do so because, in their experience, control over behaviour has been exerted by punitive or other aversive means. The counter argument is, of course, that where control is exerted by positive reinforcement, the associated emotional effects tend to be positive rather than negative. For example, those who have experienced control by being forced to participate in school sports under the threat of sanctions may regard any proposed control over their participation in a similar light.

Other critics have suggested that a Skinnerian approach to the design of a culture would not work simply because the behaviour of man is too complex. Studies with relatively simple organisms, they argue, do not provide evidence for the possibility of manipulating man in all his diversity and complexity. Skinner himself would agree that we are far from having developed a thoroughly defensible behavioural technology. The ground work and principles have been established in the laboratory setting and some applications have been made in real-life situations. These applications have been produced mainly in institutional settings where there is the possibility of exerting considerable control over the environment. It could be argued that rather than having reached the stage of implementing change, we have merely provided a good case for further research into the behavioural technology which could be applied at some time in the future. We do not yet have, perhaps, sufficient evidence on the effects of multiple reinforcers on behaviour, particularly where these vary in strength and exert control over either partially or totally incompatible responses. Nor have we yet a clear understanding of reciprocal reinforcers which are so clearly a phenomenon in everyday life. When there are clearer answers to these kinds of questions we may be in a better position to control behaviour more effectively. It should also be possible, through research into reciprocal reinforcement, to find answers to the question of who controls the controllers. The vision of man being manipulated is not a pleasant prospect within our culture, particularly since we feel that man is not manipulated at the moment. The fact that the behavioural view sees man as under the control of haphazardly arranged contingencies and that the substitution of superior planning would lead to desirable results, does little to alleviate the apprehension concerning who might occupy the position of controller. Nevertheless, Skinner has argued cogently that the mechanisms of reciprocal reinforcement should provide sufficient balance that a despotism, no matter how benevolent, need not be feared nor be a necessary component of the changes. Where decisions are made by an individual or group of individuals, we can rightly' assume that their decision-making behaviour will be as much under the control of its consequences as the behaviour of those whose behaviour is being manipulated by the decisions. Extended research into reciprocal reinforcement might provide the reassurance necessary that the mechanics of the situation justify this optimism.

If we assume that we have the capacity to develop an efficient and balanced behavioural technology, there are still some questions which cannot currently be answered. One of these arises from the view that knowledge, of itself, gives rise to changes in behaviour. Gergen (1973) has discussed this phenomenon with respect to social psychology. One of the central arguments of his paper is that the dissemination of psychological knowledge modifies the patterns of behaviour upon which the knowledge is based. Gergen (1973) makes the telling point that herein lies a fundamental difference between the natural sciences and a science of behaviour:

The (natural) scientist cannot typically communicate his knowledge to the subjects of his study such that their behavioural dispositions are modified. In the social sciences such communication can have a vital impact on behaviour.

This line of thought is relevant to the concept of behaviour modification through operant conditioning techniques in two very distinct ways. Firstly, there is the problem of the belief in autonomous man and the freedom of choice with which this view tends to be associated. Within western culture there is a current tendency to evaluate predictability in a negative fashion. The term predictable has become pejorative. Obviously, there are wide cultural variations, both historically and geographically, but it would seem true to say that in western culture at the moment the label 'predictable' can be regarded as a verbal punisher. To the extent that this is the case the dissemination of knowledge concerning reinforcement principles may result in their reduced effectiveness. Social psychologists have used the term reactance to describe this phenomenon (*see* Brehm, 1966). Reactance theory predicts that if a subject is informed that some behaviour on his part is predictable and a description of the behaviour is provided, this will result in that individual producing some alternative behaviour. This theory has been tested in numerous situations, particularly in the context of attitude change. In one study (Sensenig and Brehm, 1968) it was suggested that subjects who had already expressed an attitude on a questionnaire would change that attitude when told that a partner had already decided what their position would be in writing a short essay on that topic. Post-testing showed that those subjects significantly altered their attitudes relative to a control group. Evidence of this kind suggests that we have been reinforced in the past for non-predictable behaviours and that we have a tendency to change our behaviour when informed of predictions made about us. In any discussion of sport and the manipulation of sport's behaviour, the influence of the reactance tendency must be borne in mind. We have outlined a view of behavioural determinism which appears to be justified both by laboratory evidence and by application in real-life situations, but included in this determinism is the influence of our history of being reinforced for uniqueness. When any implementation of operant principles are made the degree to which this factor is influential is likely to have a contributing role in their success.

Gergen's (1973) article has a second ramification. This concerns the kinds of reinforcers which are available. Throughout this book it has been assumed that prestige, status and esteem are frequently encountered as significant reinforcers in the sports context. This prestige is largely dependent on the fact that the population as a whole views behaviour as a product of autonomous man. In Skinner's terminology we award credit because the controlling variables are not obvious; the success of the individual does not appear to have environmental determinants. If it is commonly accepted that there are such environmental determinants, the degree of credit awarded an individual for his behaviour may decrease. In other words, one of the most effective of the reinforcers may diminish in reinforcing capacity. If we no longer give credit to autonomous man, holding him responsible for his successes and failures, but attribute them to environmental control, the value of such credit as a reinforcer is correspondingly reduced. Two alternative paths appear to be open. The first of these is that the dissemination of information is restricted. Knowledge of the principles is restricted to those who are involved in the manipulations. In this way prestige may continue to be an effective reinforcer, since, for the majority, there has been no acceptance of behavioural determinism. This is probably neither a legitimate nor ethically acceptable method of application for it implies an elitist view of controllers and controlled and probably provides fuel for an anti-behaviourist stance. But it is probable that in any practical sense this may occur. Even without any limitation of knowledge in a planned or formal way, it is likely that only a relatively small handful of individuals would change in their reinforcing strategy. We may plan the contingencies of reinforcement through credit and esteem and find only a minority reducing the credit they award because of the determinism involved. The inertia of cultural values would at best allow this avenue of approach for some considerable period of time.

The other alternative is, of course, to seek alternative reinforcers which will maintain their effectiveness despite knowledge of their reinforcing capacity. If we can use an example for a moment, we may cite money as an obvious alternative. In the second section it was pointed out that money as a strong generalized secondary reinforcer is currently applied effectively in professional sport. The rise of professionalism can be thought of as a continuing appreciation of the value of this reinforcer. It is possible that money could substitute in many situations where credit is currently awarded. The complexity of current practices may be illustrated by pointing out that prestige or credit is also awarded for having money. How far any reduction in the value of prestige and status as reinforcers will produce a concomitant reduction in the value of money as a reinforcer is an interesting point whose impact must be the subject of research into the development of any behavioural technology with intended application. Perhaps the answer to this question lies in the development of an entirely new category of reinforcers. The acquisition of a reinforcing capacity by a neutral stimulus through association with primary reinforcers was referred to in section one. There is no reason why stimuli which we currently classify as neutral should not be developed in this manner. Provided that the regular association of this stimulus occurs with primary or other secondary reinforcers we could develop a reinforcer which was not subject to a cultural history and would serve the needs of manipulating behaviour.

Goals of a Behavioural Technology in Sport
Bearing in mind the problems associated with our currently limited state of knowledge some prescriptions concerning change can be made. There still remains the problem of the kind of behaviour that we are hoping to achieve by our manipulation. The goal will obviously depend upon the level of sport concerned in our discussion. When we consider international sport we may

choose a goal of international supremacy in sport of all kinds. Our alternative goal might be derived in terms of the individual—that our manipulation should lead to the life-long participation in some sport for every individual. There are many levels of behavioural goals possible between these two. What must be emphasized at the outset is that, even when the cautionary notes above are taken into account, the principles of behaviour modification are currently available for achievement of these objectives. These can be realized without reference to changing people's minds or 'inspiring national pride in sport' or giving people the 'will to be fit.' That is, the attributes of autonomous man are unnecessary for the modifications proposed. The degree to which we approach or succeed in these goals depends entirely on the degree to which we are prepared to conscientiously plan the contingencies of reinforcement which are necessary for their achievement.

Once a behavioural view is accepted a number of the goals currently held by physical educationists and coaches become redundant. It has already been argued in section five that the development of a positive attitude towards sport is a redundant goal. That category of behaviours which we label as an attitude is largely affected by those reinforcements available for sport itself and by the manipulation of participation in sport the other components of an attitude will also change. Frost (1971) listed twelve goals and purposes of physical education and athletic programs. Many of these simply have no meaning in a behavioural orientation toward sport. For example, two such goals are:

Testing the individual physically, emotionally, and morally through participation in vigorous and demanding competitive activities in the course of which hidden resources must be called out and courage, determination, and self-confidence may be discovered and developed.

and

Satisfying the needs for fun, relaxation, and the satisfaction of accomplishment, which are so necessary for both mental and physical health (Frost, 1971).

The idea of revealing 'hidden' resources is suggestive of latent qualities of autonomous man which can be brought to fruition in sport. In our behavioural viewpoint these qualities may be regarded as no more than aspects of behaviour which are not currently a part of the individual's repertoire. Whether these behaviours can be developed through appropriate reinforcement in sport is an interesting question. It involves the definition of the qualities in behavioural terms. Provided we can define what we mean by 'bravery' in terms of behaviour, it may be possible to manipulate it. Even if this step is taken the possibility that this kind of behaviour will appear in contexts other than the one in which they are learned is questionable and will depend on a number of generalization factors.

116

The second goal designated by Frost provides a list of some of the reinforcements for sport and some of the believed consequences of these reinforcers. It is not a goal of participation, but a specification of contingencies.

If we examine one behavioural goal in terms of interventions that are currently possible, methods of implementation can be elucidated. An objective which would be subscribed to by a large proportion of sports administrators and physical education teachers is that all those physically able to participate in sports activities should do so. Our starting point must, therefore, be that universal participation in sport is an objective which can be reached through manipulation of appropriate reinforcers.

Many of the other behavioural goals in sport would be achieved if universal participation were established. High quality of performance would be likely to result because of the increased pool of competitors. This, in turn, would produce greater success in international performances and at every level in the sporting hierarchy.

The degree to which we are prepared to adopt appropriate contingencies depends on the reinforcement those with current power to implement the changes receive for their manipulation. This power lies, of course, in part, with governments and the possibility of achieving changes in governmental behaviour with respect to sport may be limited but are nonetheless not unattainable.

Government Interventions

At this point we might examine certain hard proposals in terms of governmental intervention that could achieve universal participation. Let us assume that it would be beneficial for a nation as a whole to participate actively in some sport. One could cite the known benefits to health which accrue from this participation. The advertising campaign for participation known as 'Participaction' currently being used in Canada indicates that governments have this behavioural goal as one of their objectives even now. What is lacking in this campaign is, of course, much change in the effective reinforcers. The alternative is to provide greater tangible reinforcement for participation. Governments have in their power the means by which this can be done. Normally, we associate the exercise of this power with the use of punishment or censure. A government conventionally operates by providing sanctions against undesired behaviour—by producing laws which punish the offender. This need not be the case. We seldom see the application of positive reinforcement, simply because governments find that adequate changes in behaviour can be produced through punishment and hence they receive reinforcement for its use. In one interesting attempt at reversing this situation police in one city in the United States sent notes to people who were observed driving safely to congratulate them on their behaviour. This was staggeringly novel for many people and viewed by many as a waste of money.

In terms of participation in sport, there is an obvious source of positive reinforcement in the income tax system used so unfailingly throughout the world. Were an individual to have his tax reduced following participation in

117

sport, we should have a tangible reinforcement which a government could provide for sport. Naturally, this proposal would be met with a good deal of scepticism, but would offer an ideal vehicle for providing positive reinforcement. If the objective of a government is the promotion of positive health and the evidence supports a relationship between active participation in sport and health, then this kind of reinforcement may be a suitable way of achieving that goal.

The advantages to a government are twofold. Money currently available for sports promotion or participation in activities could be diverted to the administration of the program. The savings in terms of reduced medical costs could be an escalating reinforcer for the government to maintain its behaviour (the program). There seems ample evidence for the fact that degenerative diseases are a major source of medical expense in western civilization. This might be alleviated by such a program and the impact would be likely to grow with the longevity of the program. The economic benefits could be very much greater. The amount of working time lost through degenerative illness must be substantial although it is not known whether such statistics are available in any western societies. Since it is the under-retiring age group which should benefit from the program to the greatest extent, the contribution to a national economy may be significant.

Naturally, the practical organization of the system might take considerable planning. Since governments, we are assuming, are concerned with promoting positive health, there is no reason why the proposed system should not be developed in association with a medical checkup. For example, a simple method of implementation which would provide indirect reinforcement for sports participation would be a tax deduction for presentation at the time of tax returns of a certificate indicating a medical check-up within that fiscal year. The amount of tax relief could be doubled for an additional certification to the effect that a certain defined level of cardio-respiratory efficiency level had been achieved. This level could be determined by age or using whatever manipulations are appropriate. There exist already tests for cardio-vascular or cardio-respiratory efficiency whose objective scoring could be quite suitable for the system. Whether the tests would be run by physicians, para-medical staff or at special testing centers is again a minor obstacle.

Should such a scheme be implemented and cardio-respiratory level be adjusted appropriately it could require considerable activity for the achievement of the level at which a tax exemption could be claimed. The manipulation of reinforcement could be accomplished both in terms of amount (magnitude of tax relief) and in terms of the number of responses (level of activity) required for reinforcement to occur. One drawback, which it could be predicted may become apparent after a period of time, is that, since tax returns are made at regular annual intervals, the population would be placed on a fixed interval schedule of reinforcement. This could lead to the 'scalloping' effect noted in section one, in which frequency of responding increases as the scheduled reinforcement approaches. One could imagine a frantic pursuit of activity as the time for the annual checkup neared. It is not beyond the realm of administrative ingenuity to cause this schedule to vary, but even without manipulation the fixed interval schedule could produce sufficient change in cardio-respiratory efficiency for the program to have merits.

This example is provided more as an instance of the kinds of positively reinforcing contingencies available for use at a governmental level rather than as a specific recommendation. It has the advantage of potentially off-setting costs to the government, whereas other schemes involving secondary reinforcers, such as money, may be expensive without the benefit in terms of economic returns. In this context it is again necessary to remember that reciprocal reinforcement is available apart from economic returns. If governmental programs receive the reinforcement of vote catching, they are likely to be maintained regardless of economic viability. The fact remains, however, that reinforcement for all can be expensive and could be regarded as a failure in 'husbanding' resources or in governmental priorities. Many nations subsidize sport by the use of a very efficient schedule of reinforcement—the variable ratio schedule. Gambling is a behaviour which receives a low rate of reinforcement provided at irregular intervals. Those who have been influenced by such a schedule show a long period of responding before extinction occurs. Establishing national lotteries of various kinds and using the income to subsidize sport can reduce the cost of any program for assistance to sport by a considerable margin.

Significant changes in behaviour do not rely necessarily on the regular reinforcement of all individuals. We have already discussed the phenomenon of competition in the preceding chapter. Individuals do engage in activities in which only one of a number of contestants can receive the available reinforcement. Perhaps one could outline a simple instance in which this relatively parsimonious use of reinforcers could be applied at a governmental level. Community recreational centers or activity buildings could be provided on some kind of competitive basis. Within a particular district or country, those top four communities (or three or two communities) in terms of sports participation would receive the new building on whatever cost-sharing basis is appropriate. This could be achieved in terms of the total population or handled more effectively in terms of costs through the school system. For example, those communities with the highest proportion of children able to swim fifty yards could receive the new facility or those meeting some other specification in terms of activities. One advantage in this system is that the reinforcement to the community would contribute to the continuation of the activity. In this sense, the competition provides data indicating a need which is met by the reinforcement.

An alternative to a general competition could be a specific competition between two or three communities matched for size and along other relevant dimensions. Between these three communities the facility could be offered to that community producing superior performance in terms of activity. There is also no reason why this should not extend over years with the same kind of facility being offered in subsequent competitions to those communities who had lost in the first year. An established system of this sort could provide the reinforcement necessary, but spread the economic burden over a considerable period of time.

Perhaps these two examples are sufficient to indicate the reinforcing resources available to governments at the moment which they are failing to utilize. Planning for new facilities tends to be accomplished on the basis of population and sums of money for their construction are distributed on a demographic basis. The money is therefore available but when it is spent, it reinforces no specific behaviours. Instead, making reception of the money contingent upon activity would be influential on behaviour to a much greater extent. It is an assumption of these schemes that inherent reinforcers in the sport will maintain the behaviour once it has been established, but this need not necessarily occur and governments may decide to intervene by supplying continuing reinforcement for participation, either at an individual or at a community level.

At the individual level, the tax relief system has been discussed as one alternative. This is more akin to negative reinforcement since it involves reward through the removal of some noxious event (paying taxes), but positive reinforcers are used by governments at an individual level for other activities and could be extended within the sport context. One is conscious of the superficial anomaly which exists in many western nations where there is concern over population growth and at the same time family allowances are provided. A 'fitness allowance' would constitute direct reinforcement for participation in some activity and while it would be an expensive system, its cost could again be partially off-set in economic terms by the reduction of medical costs and the savings in lost working time.

Individual reinforcers may again be made competitive. In one way, some governments already achieve this by the use of honours lists and, in some states, the granting of sinecures. The extent to which these individual reinforcers have a significant influence on participation is probably small, since so few are ever granted. There is no reason why systems of this kind should not be extended.

Although our discussion has revolved around the application of reinforcers, governments also have it in their power to manipulate some of the aversive consequences of participation in sport. Any movement in this direction may thereby increase the value of associated positive reinforcers already available. An example may clarify this point. Currently, participation in amateur sport may be curbed at the upper levels because individuals are punished in their regular jobs by lost time. The reduction of this aversive state, through government payment of broken-time salaries, for example, would allow the positive reinforcers within the situation to be more fully influential. International amateur associations may veto this proposal, but it has behavioural merits in the achievement of goals of participation.

The governing bodies of sports have it within their power to perform similar functions. They may publish their own honours lists from within the sport, develop monetary rewards for aspects of behaviour of individuals within the sport of which they approve. Many such organizations are also engaged in promoting the sport amongst the young, where they hope to find new recruits. This could lead to an emphasis on those reinforcing aspects of the sport for the individual and a reduction of the aversive aspects during the early stages. No doubt this kind of control is currently exerted by governing bodies to a greater or lesser extent. It is argued here, however, that making the goal explicit and identifying those reinforcers which currently exert an influence is required for the methods to gain optimal results.

The nature of the available reinforcers will vary from sport to sport as do the associated aversive contingencies. The degree to which these may be enhanced and decreased respectively for the neophyte is also variable. Once the stimuli have been categorized explicitly, the governing body may be able to manipulate the introductory environment in a way which is conducive to increased participation. This is a reverse of the 'Throw them in at the deep end' philosophy and is supported by the behavioural evidence. Through such manipulation the novice may have developed a very strong tendency to continue his behaviour before the inherent punishers within the sport are introduced to him. At that point the influence of the aversive stimuli may be reduced since the tendency to continue his responding will more than compensate for an occasional aversive event. This is no doubt current within many sports already.

Coaches, teachers and governing bodies already design training programs in which the aversive consequences of participation are minimized. For example, instructors' manuals for teaching swimming emphasize that the young learner should not be exposed to frightening stimulus situations, if this can be avoided. In sports of this kind the problem is obvious and relatively easily manipulated, but there exist aversive events in other sports which are regarded so much as 'part of the sport' that alternative training approaches have not been tried.

The School System

Perhaps an even greater responsibility for developing this method of introducing sports rests with the schools. At a specific level the acquisition of the behaviour with continuous positive reinforcement and only subsequent introduction of the aversive aspects should lead to increased participation. Education has depended for so long on control via aversive means that such a project would require considerable change in its implementation. The notion of compulsory participation in physical education classes backed by aversive sanctions available within the school system has had a long history and there have been relatively few dissenting voices. However, it is clear that compulsory participation alone does not lead to the development of a long lasting tendency to participate. Instead, the experiences when they have been aversive, may lead to a much greater tendency to avoid any such contact with sport in the future. In recognition of this problem some solutions have already been tried. The development of modern educational gymnastics can be viewed in this way. Having identified success or 'achievement' as a significant reinforcer of activity, the modern educational gymnasts have suggested that all may 'achieve' or be successful if their performance is neither measured against an external referent nor against

121

peers' performances but against a self-determined level of previous performance.

This view then demands that the teachers act as the reinforcing agent and provide secondary reinforcers such as praise when some previous standard has been surpassed. In hypothetical terms this system sounds like a sound application of behavioural principles. There are a number of problems associated with this technique which become obvious on closer inspection. Firstly, there is the problem of establishing behavioural goals when no external standards are applied. This may be accomplished only by a teacher setting exacting standards for himself in terms of observation which may not be practical in a school setting. When dealing with perhaps thirty or more children at any one time, the reinforcement of appropriate behaviour may be haphazard at best simply because the teacher cannot observe all children with accuracy. A second factor is the fact that within the social setting of such a lesson, there are opportunities for comparison with others in spite of the self-standard set by the teacher. A child may still fail and have this communicated verbally or non-verbally to him by his peers despite the reinforcement of the teacher. This aversive stimulation may be less potent an influence when the child is young, but may serve to off-set the reinforcement of the most assiduous observer amongst teachers. It is generally acknowledged that the potential reinforcing power of the peer group relative to the power of adults increases with age.

Achievement, in the behavioural view, is no more than the emotional parallels of receiving certain positive reinforcers for particular kinds of responses. Within this culture, those responses which receive this kind of reinforcement are mainly competitive and particularly so within sport and activity. To suggest that it is possible to manipulate the emotional concomitants by redefining achievement in terms of arbitrarily set standards which are not comparative but personal, is probably beyond the scope of the individual teacher. In order to accomplish this shift, a cultural redefinition of reinforcing contingencies would have to be developed. These in turn would probably reduce the reinforcement for those specifically competitive kinds of sports and would therefore serve to reduce the reinforcement for what is a major aspect of sport as a phenomenon.

A second aspect of the school system is the compulsory nature of participation. In a behavioural analysis this must be likened to an active avoidance training situation. In experimental terms, an organism can avoid some noxious stimulus by producing a particular response. The behaviour is often said to be maintained on the basis of secondary negative reinforcers. Behaviour continues, in non technical jargon, on the basis of fear of punishment. While this type of contingency can produce both high levels of responding and lengthy resistance to extinction, it only occurs when the organism is forcibly replaced into the experimental situation. Where any opportunity is provided for total avoidance of the whole context, this opportunity will be taken. If we observe behaviour in school children, this phenomenon is striking. Every teacher in physical education knows of those in his classes who would immediately produce alternative behaviours once the sanctions were lifted. If active avoidance is the major force at work in maintaining behaviour, the relatively mild positive reinforcers of which the teacher is capable become useless. In terms of the stimulus control of behaviour, one may liken the teacher in this situation to a stimulus with which avoidance responses have become associated. In addition there are likely to be emotional correlates which may transfer to new sports situations. One effect of the 'teacher as stimulus for avoidance' is that his capacity as a positive reinforcer is also reduced. If the teacher provides positive reinforcement, he is likely to become a secondary reinforcer of himself. (Our definition of a secondary reinforcer was of an initially neutral stimulus continually associated with positive reinforcement.) When the teacher is associated with punishment, this reinforcing capacity is lost.

These observations imply that a reorganization is essential to promote not only participation in sport in schools but also continued participation after the school career. There are several alternatives. The first of these is an elitist view with which the majority may not find sympathy. This system would remove compulsion from the physical education program and concentrate on developing the highest possible levels of performance of those who voluntarily enter the program. This system would mean that no avoidance tendencies were developed during the school years for those who did not voluntarily participate. They would then perhaps be more likely to be influenced by the positive reinforcers available for after-school participation. The disadvantage of this proposal is that it rejects the contention that the maintenance of positive health depends on regular exercise during the school years. The accuracy of this contention, which is an assumption upon which the compulsory system is based, has not been tested empirically so far as the author is aware. Test projects involving voluntary participation only, might reveal some interesting aspects of the impact of current mandatory activity.

This proposal maintains the current status of positive reinforcement for performance. Whatever secondary reinforcers are provided by peers and the teacher continue to be available and those awards, distinctions and credit provided through the school system for superior performance remain unaltered. One may, however, arrange to supplement the positive reinforcement currently available and so add to the probable participation level. This may be achieved within the voluntary system proposed, as an additional manipulation or it may be applied to the current compulsory system. That is, an alternative proposed may be that the current system be maintained, but that the magnitude and frequency of positive reinforcement be increased. This is an attempt to off-set the negative aspects of compulsory performance by a counteracting increase in positive reinforcement. This may be accomplished within an existing framework by increases in magnitude of current reinforcers. There is, however, an alternative in terms of the introduction of entirely new reinforcement systems. Privilege systems are often easily established in schools and may be manipulated as reinforcement for superior performance.

The major problem associated with a system of this kind is that there remains the possibility that those who cannot prove superior in competition against others will still receive no reinforcement. Whether this is the result of the individual's history of reinforcement or the result of a genetically determined factor, it remains the case that in a competitive situation, some individuals will be unreinforced. Where novel tangible reinforcers are introduced it is possible that objectively set personal standards could be used. For example, a percentage increase in level of performance for an individual may result in the privilege being awarded, despite a low absolute value. The difference between this system and that recommended by the modern educational gymnasts is that the standards are set objectively and reinforcement is contingent upon their accomplishment.

It should be emphasized that an absence of compulsion does not imply permissiveness. This has been offered as a solution to problems created by sanctions, but a permissive approach has little to recommend it from the behavioural standpoint:

> Permissive practices have many advantages. They save the labour of supervision and the enforcement of sanctions. They do not generate counterattack. . . . Permissiveness is not, however, a policy; it is the abandonment of policy, and its apparent advantages are illusory. To refuse to control is to leave control not to the person himself, but to other parts of the social and nonsocial environments (Skinner, 1971).

The objective is to remove the punitive contingencies, so much a part of the school environment, and yet maintain control of behaviour through non-aversive means. If control is abrogated to the rest of the 'social and nonsocial environment' we are no further ahead in achieving the behavioural objectives.

One aspect of all school behaviour which is difficult to deal with by manipulations of the school environment is the similarity between the school and extra-school reinforcement contingencies. We pointed out in section three that a number of reinforcing agencies may have a significant influence on a person at any given time. If a child is reinforced for not participating in sport by his parents and given positive reinforcement for statements against sport, he is likely to bring this tendency to respond to school or to find that a competition exists between tendencies to respond. In some ways this may not constitute a problem. The stimulus control of behaviour may lead to different responses occurring in the different situations. For example, adolescent boys are usually reinforced for swearing amongst their peer group and swear frequently. The same boys may seldom or never swear at home where the same behaviour is punished. It is possible that behaviour with respect to sport may be influenced in similar fashion. Social psychologists have a tendency to label the phenomenon as 'role playing.' This can be viewed from a behavioural stance as a simple aspect of stimulus control. When one tendency has been strongly developed, however, there remains the possibility of relatively weaker reinforcers for opposite responses having little effect on behaviour. We have also concluded that there is some tendency for people to be reinforced for consistency in their behaviour. It is probable that a resolution of these opposing tendencies may favour the individual responding in a manner contradictory to the reinforcement contingencies developed by the school. There is no way to circumvent this problem except by a change at a cultural level. One is aware, for example, that in boarding schools where the control of the environment is greater, there is apparently a higher level of homogeneity of behaviour developed amongst the children. Diversity is promoted within a day school system because of the competing reinforcement contingencies available outside the school.

One current development in physical education which appears soundly based in behavioural terms is the development of options in participation for children. Since there are inherent reinforcers and punishers in sports and since genetic endowment is likely to determine, in part, the potential for reinforcement for an individual in a specific sport, it is conceivable that a greater proportion of children will discover the sport in which they receive a higher proportion of reinforcement when they are exposed to a large number of sports. It would appear that choice of sports is a factor of considerable importance in establishing participation. There are, however, two problems with which choice becomes associated. Firstly, there are so many sports that some arbitrary selection becomes necessary. Even presupposing that a reasonable criterion for selection can be established, the question of number of sports becomes extremely difficult to determine. If we remember that many sports only provide significant reinforcement after a high level of skill has been achieved, in providing exposure to a large number of sports each sampled briefly, there is a possibility that the child will never experience the inherent reinforcers available in that sport. A good example of this is the game of tennis where a fairly extensive training and participating process is necessary before one does more than the tedious repetition of lifting the balls out of the net. Whenever a restriction in number is made in order to pursue a sport in depth, there is a probability that the particular sport for which an individual has a high level of potential will never be tried.

The above analysis presupposes that a 'free' choice is available only after a certain compulsory exposure of a number of sports. This is not the case in many current uses of this system. A choice is sometimes given without prior experience. It is in this sense that the choice is labelled as 'free.' What must be understood is that the selection of the sport is then made on the basis of preceding contingencies of reinforcement associated with sports as a whole. The choice is not 'free' but is determined by the influence of the child's history of reinforcement or punishment associated with similar situations. Those reinforcing contingencies which have emerged from the socialization process of the child are likely to dictate what selection of response is made by the child. Absence of control results in a reliance on fortuitous preceding controlling events. It is possible, for example, that a high proportion of children will select those sports which are dominant within their culture, simply because they are the sports which receive the greatest magnitude of reinforcement in the outside world. Alternatively, those sports for which older siblings receive reinforcement may be selected. This process becomes as arbitrary as the selection of sports made by the teacher and the probability of the child encountering those sports which maximize his positive reinforcement is just as low. Another problem of 'free' choice also becomes apparent where the child brings to the selection process a previously established tendency toward avoidance. Previous aversive experience of some kind may have resulted in a tendency to avoid the sport situation, or positive reinforcement for avoidance behaviour has resulted in the same tendency. This will lead to the least sports-like activity being selected. The author remembers that as an undergraduate his university had a system of compulsory physical activity on a one hour per week basis for freshmen. Those in the 'avoidance category' tended to find their way into table-tennis classes, which were very frequently rather idle ping-pong sessions. While many students chose new sports which they had never encountered and received reinforcement for these, the avoidance group constituted a sizable minority. Equally, the compulsory nature of the system made it a prime target for student demands for administrative change within the university.

In this section we have considered some of the problems associated with achieving the goal of universal participation. There are additional goals to which we may now turn.

Coaching

The process of acquiring skill was examined in section four and in that section a number of points concerning the behaviour of the coach were elaborated.

The primary area for change in the manipulation of reinforcers lies in the behaviour of the coaches. In this context it is the detail of performance with a particular skill which is important and not so much the participation or non-participation of the individual in sport as a whole. It is usually regarded as the coach's responsibility to develop skill as efficiently as possible and there are several areas in which the behavioural principles become important. One rationale for the assumption that the rapid development of skill is the coach's responsibility is that such development of the skill is likely to mean that higher levels of reinforcement may be achieved relatively quickly. A lengthy acquisition process is likely to mean that, in many sports, the maintenance of participation depends on relatively weak extrinsic reinforcers until inherent or intrinsic reinforcement becomes available.

An additional point with respect to the behaviour of the coach which is very frequently forgotten is that he is also a behaving organism whose performance is manipulated by its contingencies. In recommending particular strategies of behaviour for the coach to follow it is often extremely difficult for these to be executed if this is not considered too. For example, where long-term goals may be achieved by a strategy of coaching which has little immediate success, we are asking the coach to tolerate long delays of reinforcement. This may result in the extinction of his behaviour before the goal is reached. Similarly, we may recommend that a coach should not use aversive stimulation for the modification of a player's behaviour. The evidence from studies of punishment show that avoidance tendencies are likely to be developed in this way. Additionally, it is very possible that since the coach himself is a stimulus to the player, that his dispensing of aversive stimulation may result in the coach being able to act as a less effective positive reinforcer on subsequent occasions. However, aversive stimulation may bring about a rapid and significant improvement in the performance of the player. This will constitute an immediate reinforcement for the coach, hence making this kind of behaviour more probable in the future and further reducing his capacity to act as a positive reinforcer. In essence, it is possible to establish a vicious circle of coaching behaviour resulting in ultimate reduced effectiveness. In summary, when we become aware of the reciprocal reinforcements existing between coach and performer it becomes very much less easy to be dogmatic concerning coaching strategies.

The range of behaviours with which coaches are associated is also of fundamental significance to any prescriptions for coaching behaviour. Very few coaches, for example, see their charges develop from absolute novice all the way to their ultimate level of performance. At the lower levels of skill the characteristics of skilled performance are likely to take a major part of the coaching effort. In this situation the coach is going to be concerned with shaping behaviour in the development of basic skills. In order to accomplish this with maximal efficiency the coach should know the optimum size of behavioural steps which can be achieved. In other words, the coach must so divide the total skill that a progression is achieved with reinforcement available for each successive approximation to the desired behaviour. One problem associated with this interpretation of the behavioural approach is that there are likely to exist reinforcers for the novice apart from those provided by the coach for the complete performance at a low level, rather than superior performance for parts of the skill. Some combination of the two approaches may result in optimizing total reinforcement and result in higher probability of continued participation even though this procedure may not be optimum for speed of learning in terms of total acquisition of the skill. For example, in many teams game situations fundamental supportive skills exist whose acquisition is essential for performance. It is logical from the coach's standpoint that these be acquired first. The child may find that the reinforcers available for playing the game itself are more influential and more likely to maintain behaviour. There are those coaches in ice hockey, for example, who recommend a progression from learning to skate, to learning to stick-handle, to learning to body-check, to the final game. Yet reinforcement from peers and parents is directed towards performance in games and not in practice.

A combination of practice plus games seems the reasonable way to optimize both efficiency in acquisition and continued participation. There is an additional problem involved in practice, however, and one of which coaches are becoming increasingly aware. We noted in section one that those stimulus conditions under which a response is reinforced tend to elicit that response on future occasions. The phenomenon of stimulus control is of relevance to the acquisition of sport skill in the context of practice versus game play. If the conditions under which practice occurs differ dramatically from those under which the game is played, the benefit of that practice is severely curtailed. A skilled response acquired when no opponent is present may be disrupted when the new dimension of competition is introduced. Coaches have already become aware that training for a sports skill should occur in simulated game situations which in a behavioural analysis implies a high level of similarity between the sets of stimulus conditions.

One aspect of the coach's behaviour which can be manipulated is his capacity to schedule the reinforcements he provides. Superior acquisition is likely to occur if successive approximations to the desired behaviour are provided with continuous reinforcement. Initial acquisition, however, is not always the prime concern. After the skill is acquired its maintenance or strengthening is better accomplished with some form of partial reinforcement. If highest levels of responding are required, variable interval and variable ratio schedules are often used in order to develop consistent high-level responding. In one way the coach's behaviour may be in conflict with other reinforcers. If he reduces the frequency with which a response is reinforced after it has been acquired, the general public or peers may increase its frequency of reinforcement as the level of the skill increases. The advantage of the coach's behaviour is therefore likely to be minimized at later stages, but to be of greatest significance during the acquisition phase.

An additional limitation on the direct application of a behavioural technology concerns the topography of responding. In using frequency of responding as a major measure of performance in operant conditioning, the details of the movement are of little concern. On the other hand, these are likely to be of paramount importance in a sports skill. In this context the question of fatigue during training is critical. If the performer begins to become fatigued during the execution of his skill, the topography of the response is likely to vary. Some of these variations may result in less effective performance. If reinforcement from the coach persists, it is likely that the inappropriate movements will be learned and hence result in the acquisition of poor behaviour. Alternatively, criticism or other verbal punishers may have an impact on overall tendency to perform. The performance in training of any skill which is well learned, under conditions of fatigue is therefore to be deprecated.

Where coaches have somewhat limited secondary reinforcers only at their disposal, it is probable that they may also lose some of their effectiveness over lengthy periods of training. It was noted in section one that a reinforcer may depend on the state of deprivation of the animal for its effectiveness. During experimentation, the animal's level of deprivation is maintained so that satiation does not occur despite the reinforcements. Transsituational secondary reinforcers may function independently of the state of deprivation of the organism. However, in real life situations the reinforcers of attention or praise may lose some of their effectiveness as controllers of behaviour as some process equivalent to satiation occurs. Lengthy practice sessions are more likely to engender this result than shorter sessions. It is possible that much of the contradictory evidence concerning schedules of practice in motor learning is a result of this phenomenon rather than a function of any inherent aspect of the learning system.

Summary
It has been argued in this section that sport is an aspect of behaviour within Western culture which can be manipulated. At different levels within the hierarchy of sport, manipulations of reinforcement and punishment may be used in achieving behavioural goals. Governments, governing bodies of sports, educators and coaches currently exert sufficient control over the environment for dramatic changes in level and quality of participation to be made. Many of the suggestions for manipulations are starting points, intended as stimulants to discussion and research. It is also true that many of the suggestions which have been made currently form a part of the activities of these controllers. The suggestions are made with full awareness that many of the authorities with power are already following the proposals or modifications of them. Their reiteration has been made in order to demonstrate that the proposals can be derived directly from a Skinnerian analysis of behaviour.

In the preface to this work it was noted that sport psychology has developed to the stage where eclectism has become common. This book is not part of that trend and has presented a single psychological view of a number of related aspects of sport. It should be emphasized that many points raised within this book are speculation. Only when the necessary empirical research has occurred will it be possible to provide firm proposals for the modification of behaviour.

References

ADAMS, J.A. (1966). Some mechanisms of motor responding: An examination of attention. In E.A. Bilodeau [Ed.]. *Acquisition of Skill.* New York: Academic Press.

ADLER, A. (1927). *The Practice and Theory of Individual Psychology.* New York: Harcourt Brace and World.

ANNETT, J. (1959). Learning a pressure under conditions of immediate and delayed knowledge of results. *Quarterly Journal of Experimental Psychology,* 11, 3-15.

BAISINGER, J. & ROBERTS, D.L. (1972). Reduction of intraspecies aggression in rats by positive reinforcement of incompatible behavior. *Journal of the Experimental Analysis of Behavior,* 18, 535-40.

BILODEAU, I. McD. (1966). Information feedback. In E.A. Bilodeau, [Ed.], *Acquisition of Skill.* New York: Academic Press.

BREHM, J. (1966). *A Theory of Psychological Reactance.* New York: Academic Press.

CATTELL, R. (1965). *The Scientific Analysis of Personality.* Baltimore: Penguin.

EVANS, R.I. (1968). *B.F. Skinner: The Man and His Ideas.* New York: E.P. Dutton and Co., Inc.

EYSENCK, H.J. (1965). *Fact and Fiction in Psychology.* Harmondsworth: Penguin.

FITTS, P.M. (1966). Cognitive aspects of information processing: III Set for speed versus accuracy. *Journal of Experimental Psychology,* 69, 849-957.

FLEISHMAN, E.A. (1966). Human abilities and the acquisition of skill. In E.A. Bilodeau [Ed.]. *Acquisition of Skill.* New York: Academic Press.

FLEISHMAN, E.A. & RICH, S, (1963). Role of kinesthetic and spatial visual abilities in perceptual motor learning. *Journal of Experimental Psychology,* 66, 6-11.

FROST, R.B. (1971). *Psychological Concepts Applied to Physical Education and Coaching.* Reading, Mass.: Addison-Wesley.

GERGEN, K.J. (1973). Social psychology as history. *Journal of Personality and Social Psychology.* 26, 309-20.

HEFFERLINE, R.F., KEENAN, B., & HARFORD, R.A. (1959). Escape and avoidance conditioning in human subjects without their observation of the response. *Science,* 130, 1338-9.

HOLDING, D.H. (1965). *Principles of Training.* Oxford: Pergamon Press.

HOWELL, M.L. (1956). Use of force-time graphs for performance analysis in facilitating motor learning. *Research Quarterly,* 27, 12-22.

JENSEN, A.R. (1973). Skinner and human differences. In H. Wheeler [Ed.], *Beyond the Punitive Society.* San Francisco: Freeman.

JOHNSTON, M.S., KELLEY, C.S., HARRIS, F.F., & WOLF, M.M. (1966). An application of reinforcement principles to development of motor skills of a young child. *Child Development,* 37, 379-87.

KANE, J.E. (1972). Personality, body concept and performance. In J.E. Kane [Ed.], *Psychological Aspects of Physical Education and Sport.* London: Routledge and Kegan Paul.

KNAPP, B.N. (1963). *Skill in Sport.* London: Routledge and Kegan Paul.

LOGAN, F.A. (1969). *Fundamentals of Learning and Motivation.* Dubuque: Wm. C. Brown.

MARTENS, R. (1969). Effect of an audience on learning and performance of a complex motor skill. *Journal of Personality and Social Psychology,* 12, 252-60.

McCLELLAND, D.C. (1961). *The Achieving Society.* Princeton van Nostrand.

NEWCOMB, T.M. (1943). *Personality and Social Change.* New York: Holt Rinehart and Winston.

PLATT, J.R. (1973). The Skinnerian revolution. In J.H. Wheeler, [Ed.], *Beyond the Punitive Society.* San Francisco: Freeman.

REYNOLDS, G.S. (1968). *A Primer of Operant Conditioning.* Glenview, Ill.: Scott, Foresman and Co.

ROZYNKO, V., SWIFT, K., SWIFT, J. & BOGGS, L.J. (1973). Controlled environments for social change. In J.H. Wheeler, [Ed.], *Beyond the Punitive Society.* San Francisco: Freeman.

SENSENIG, J. & BREHM, J. (1968). Attitude change from an applied threat to attitudinal freedom. *Journal of Personality and Social Psychology,* 8, 324-30.

SKINNER, B.F. (1948). *Walden Two.* New York: MacMillan.

SKINNER, B.F. (1953). *Science and Human Behavior.* London, Collier-MacMillan.

SKINNER, B.F. (1971). *Beyond Freedom and Dignity,* New York: Alfred A. Knopf.

SLUSHER, H. (1967). *Man, Sport and Existence.* Philadelphia: Lea & Febiger.

SUTTON-SMITH, B. (1961). Cross-cultural study of children's games. *Yearbook of the American Philosophical Society.*

WHITING, H.T.A. (1968). *Acquiring Ball Skill:* a psychological interpretation. London: Bell.

WHITING, H.T.A. (1972). Psychology of competition. In H.T.A. Whiting [Ed.], *Readings in Sports Psychology.* London: Kimpton.

WITKIN, H.A. et al. (1962). *Psychological Differentiation.* New York: Wiley.

YOUNG, O.G. (1954). Rate of learning in relation to spacing of practice periods in archery and badminton. *Research Quarterly,* 25, 231-43.

ZAJONC, R.B. (1965). Social Facilitation. *Science,* 149, 269-74.

ZANDER, A.F. (1974). Productivity and group success: Team spirit vs. the individual achiever. *Psychology Today,* 8, 64-9.

Index

133